The Beatles didn't just happen. They were molded into the most sensational rock group in the world by the promotional genius of their enigmatic manager, Brian Epstein. When Epstein died in 1967, the magical chemistry of that group broke down.

APPLE TO THE CORE

is the unsparing inside story of the Beatles' ascent to fame under Epstein's management and their tragic decline in the hands of their subsequent guardians. It is the story of how greed, ambition, business rivalries, and petty jealousies broke up the Beatles forever.

D0710882

APPLE TO THE CORE
is an original POCKET BOOK edition.

Apple to the Core
The Unmaking of the Beatles

by Peter McCabe
and Robert D. Schonfeld

PUBLISHED BY POCKET BOOKS NEW YORK

APPLE TO THE CORE

POCKET BOOK edition published August, 1972
5th printing......................January, 1976

L

This original POCKET BOOK edition is printed from brand-new plates made from newly set, clear, easy-to-read type. POCKET BOOK editions are published by POCKET BOOKS, a division of Simon & Schuster, Inc., 630 Fifth Avenue, New York, N.Y. 10020. Trademarks registered in the United States and other countries.

Author's Note

The preparation of this project inevitably acquired some of the characteristics of its subject, most visibly an occasional visit of madness. Our unreserved thanks to the following people for their time, unselfish assistance and the benefit of their guidance.

In New York: Nat Weiss, Sid Bernstein, Blair Sabol, Lillian Roxon, Dina Karabell, Don Johnston, Arthur Gelb, Michael Kramer and Herb Corsack.

In London: Derek Taylor, Neil Aspinall, Wendy Moger, Tony Barrow, Geoffrey Ellis, John Donbar, John Morris, Chris O'Dell, William Low and Ann Sullivan.

For unqualified generosity and love: Alvin Schonfeld and Fanny M. Jordan.

For technical assistance and inspiration: Michael T. Hull, Peter and Susan van Berg and Jeffrey Oppenheim.

For comic relief and general good feeling: Arthur Levine.

Special thanks to Stella Shamoon of the London *Daily Telegraph* for her major contribution to the Northern Songs chapter.

To the children of rock.
God bless and help them.

P.M.

For Norman Retchin, whom I
miss very much.

R.D.S.

Values in pounds have been converted into their dollar equivalencies throughout this book based on the pound at $2.40, except in cases where the pound value is contained in an essential quote.

Cast of Characters

John Lennon, ex Beatle.

Paul McCartney, ex Beatle.

George Harrison, ex Beatle.

Ringo Starr, ex Beatle.

Brian Epstein, Beatles' first manager.

Allen Klein, President of ABKCO Industries Inc., business manager for John Lennon, George Harrison and Ringo Starr.

Lee Eastman, Partner in New York law firm, Eastman and Eastman. Paul McCartney's father-in-law.

John Eastman, son of Lee Eastman.

Linda Eastman, daughter of Lee Eastman, Paul McCartney's wife.

Yoko Ono, avant-garde artiste, John Lennon's second wife.

Queenie Epstein, Brian Epstein's mother.

Clive Epstein, Brian Epstein's brother.

Dick James, Managing Director of Beatles' first music publishing firm, Northern Songs.

Sir Joseph Lockwood, Chairman of E.M.I. Ltd.

Sir Lew Grade, Chairman of Associated Television (ATV).

Leonard Richenberg, Managing Director of Triumph Investment Trust Ltd.

Nat Weiss, attorney and close friend of Brian Epstein.

Prologue

Once upon a time in a faraway land, there lived an ordinary goose who was very unhappy. Nobody loved it and it did want very much to be loved. One day a kindly farmer passing by espied the animal. He thought: "What a fine-looking goose that is! I should like to have it." The goose, delighted with the farmer's affections, ran happily toward him.

The farmer fed the goose his best grain every day. Before long it grew into a very beautiful bird, which, the kindly farmer discovered, had magical powers. It began to lay many golden eggs, so many that the farmer had to build a bigger coop to hold them all. Villagers came from miles around to view the magnificent goose. The kindly farmer told them that the goose laid golden eggs because its happiness was perfect and love was its most important food. The villagers accepted the word of the wise farmer and gave the goose all their love.

But soon the farmer was tired. He had no more love left to give the goose and he needed to rest. One night after his chores, he lay down on his bunk to sleep, never to awaken.

The goose continued to lay golden eggs, unaware that its friend and keeper was gone. The eggs piled up in the coop and some of the farmhands began taking them for themselves. The goose took little notice; it just laid more and more eggs, the only thing it had learned to do. The pile of eggs diminished more quickly, until eventually there were hardly any left.

Just as the goose was thinking "Whatever shall I do?" there came along several men. Among them was a stocky, plump character in peasant garb and a tall, distinguished gentleman in a long, smart coat. Each man told the goose it must protect its eggs, especially from the other men. "Oh dear, oh dear," it thought, "this is a nasty situation." One part wanted to trust the humble-seeming little man, another part aspired to the finery of the tall man, still a third part was most concerned about the safety of the remaining eggs and a fourth part didn't care very much what happened. The villagers kept their distance, but watched with interest what took place on the farm.

One dark night before the goose had decided what to do, a group of men snuck up behind the coop. They slit the goose's belly quick as a flash and extended their hands to catch the pile of eggs which they expected to fall from the goose. Instead, there spewed forth a tangle of bloody insides which stained their hands.

The small, plump man had wanted to sell the eggs and use the profits to make his own farm bigger. He tried to sew the goose up, but was only partly successful. The eggs were never quite the same. They came out streaked with tin and so they always will.

Apple
to the Core

CHAPTER ONE

Riches Back to Rags

Two weeks before George Harrison's momentous Madison Square Garden concert in aid of the refugees of Bangladesh, his manager, Allen Klein, received a most unexpected luncheon invitation. Lord Harlech, the former British ambassador to the United States, and a close friend of the widowed Jacqueline Kennedy, had asked the most controversial personality in the pop music business to dine with him at the House of Lords. Allen Klein, whose turbulent career had only taken him across the Hudson River from Newark to New York, had probably never dreamed he would be invited to visit the Upper Chamber of the British Parliament, let alone dine there, so naturally he was delighted with the invitation.

1

Klein had not long returned from a visit to England, a visit which had ended very unpleasantly for him. For several weeks his name had been splashed across the headlines of the British papers during the case of McCartney vs. the other three Beatles. Finally, he was defeated by the appointment of a receiver, replacing him as manager of the Beatles' coveted partnership assets. Klein had not been feeling well disposed toward either the British judiciary or the British press, from whom he had received several well-aimed clouts. Nor was he held in very high regard by the British establishment, so a privileged invitation like this from such a distinguished host came as a welcome surprise. Klein was determined to take the utmost advantage of the meeting.

Lord Harlech had first met the Beatles in February 1964, when he threw a reception in their honor at the British embassy in Washington. Some of the guests on that occasion, tippling a little too heavily in the champagne, had succumbed to a raging epidemic of Beatlemania and had tried to retain mementos of Beatle hair. Relations between the group and the British Foreign Office had been strained for a while, but despite the embarrassing incident Lord Harlech evidently had remained a Beatlemaniac. The former ambassador now had a stern question to put to Allen Klein. Why was George Harrison's concert being staged in the United States, and not in England?

"I told 'im!" snapped Klein with his customary nasal bluntness. "I told 'im, 'ferchrissakes, ya country hasn't been very nice to the Beatles, not very nice at all.' Ya see, Harlech didn't like the concert bein' staged in New York. He'd even asked McCartney to do one in England. So I told 'im, 'Okay, we'll do a concert in England, a benefit for Shelter. But I want two things. I want Lennon and Harrison's drug convictions crushed. Get the drug laws changed so that first offenders get conditional discharges, retroactive. [The convictions give the two Beatles visa problems.] And another thing. I wanna ruling on Apple to see if it comes under Section 487 of the British tax laws. Yes or no, 'cause if it does, they might as well move outta the country. Why should anyone wanna stay in England with that tax situation?' "

2

Klein's harangue about his bold, single-handed crusade to persuade the British government to revise its drug laws was suddenly interrupted by the telephone. Klein was about to be offered another political contact. Senator Edward Kennedy's office wanted tickets for George's concert.

"Eh!" yelped Klein, momentarily rattled. "Er, no, tell 'em we're all sold out." The secretary apparently couldn't believe her ears. The telephone rang a second time.

"Absolutely not!" Klein blurted and slammed down the phone. "He wants to participate. What did Teddy Kennedy ever do for rock?" Klein gave a little shrug of his sloping shoulders, accompanied by a sudden shudder of the head, as if he were a recently awakened sleeper trying to shake off the lingering memory of a bad dream.

". . . So anyway, I told Harlech, 'If you can do that, we'll do a concert at Wembley Stadium.' Do you know how much money that would make? A hundred and ten thousand people! Madison Square Garden, why it's just a dry run."

Lord Harlech now knew the terms. The former British diplomat was left to ponder these impossible demands at his leisure while Klein flew to Spain for one of his rare vacations, which as usual consisted of more work than rest. Ringo's movie *Blind Man* was being filmed in Almería, and his manager had a part as a Mexican bandit. But Klein didn't allow acting to interfere with his usual occupation—wheeling and dealing. A large contingent of British journalists had been invited to watch the filming and they had to be entertained. There was little opportunity for Allen Klein to sun his stocky figure on his yacht before he had to return to New York for the big event.

The news of an impending Beatle concert had broken earlier than anticipated. George had let slip to New York *Post* columnist, Al Aronowitz, that he'd been asked to do a benefit by Ravi Shankar. Aronowitz rushed the story to print and, in getting his exclusive, had so angered Klein's staff that he placed his own concert tickets in jeopardy. But the story was out. The New York FM disc jockeys did the rest, whipping up rumors about who might appear with Harrison. Almost immediately Ringo announced he would "sit in." Eric Clapton and Leon Russell said they

3

would be there. John Lennon was a strong possibility, so was Mick Jagger, and of course the biggest question mark hung over the head of Paul McCartney. For a while it seemed certain that there would be at least three Beatles at Madison Square. Then, two days before the concert, a sudden seizure of paranoia sent Lennon tearing back to the sanctuary of his Ascot estate. George, meanwhile, had managed to contact Paul, but the renegade Beatle wanted to strike bargains. He would play only if the other three agreed to dissolve the partnership.

These disappointments didn't faze Allen Klein in the least. He rubbed his hands, chuckled to himself and despite endless hours of discussions and planning, enjoyed his new role as a concert producer, playing out the part in grandiose style. He called a press conference for George, excluded the underground papers as unworthy and haughtily told *Life* Magazine it could have an exclusive only if George appeared on the cover. *Life*'s editors were not pleased. They made sure Klein's name didn't appear in the concert write-up.

Klein claimed that his company, ABKCO Industries, would make nothing from the event. All proceeds, including those from the album and the film of the concert, would go to East Pakistan's refugees. But some of the Utopian spirit of the occasion seemed lost on Allen Klein, who was scheming to use concert events such as this to enhance his own stature and make Paul McCartney and his in-laws, the Eastman family, seem like losers after all. Klein was still smarting from the public rap on the knuckles he'd taken from a British judge when the Beatles' partnership was placed in receivership. It was the Eastmans and McCartney who had engineered this feat; now, he hoped, it would be their turn to look small.

"You know what'll happen at Wembley?" Klein mused wickedly. "George will announce he's gonna do a concert, right? About two weeks before, Ringo will say, 'Hey, I'll play too.' Then John says he's gonna be there. Everyone will wanna know where Paul is. He'll think I'm tryin' to embarrass him. You betcha, I'll roast his fuckin' ass."

So saying, Allen Klein plunged into making George's Madison Square Garden concert the most glittering "dry run" New York rock fans had ever witnessed. George phoned across the country, gathering musicians, and the ensemble grew into a rock orchestra. Crowds lined up for tickets seventy-two hours before they were due to go on sale. The box office was forced to open a day early because the line had grown to such a length. Within two hours of opening, not a ticket was left. Two 20,000 sell-outs.

On a rainy August evening, almost as many desperate ticket hunters gathered outside the Garden. The streets of New York's East Village were safe for the first time in years, as its inhabitants abandoned their territory and congregated at the Garden. But frantic efforts to gate-crash were largely frustrated, as four police checkpoints proved almost impossible to penetrate. Scalpers' prices escalated to several hundred dollars a ticket.

Alongside the youngsters without tickets stood equally disappointed button and pennant salesmen, whose bundles of paraphernalia reading WE LUV YOU BEATLES were scoffed at and ignored. The hustlers failed to realize that this was not a screaming, frenzied mob, such as graced the Beatles' appearances in 1964. This audience wanted to hear good music.

Rock had barely survived a long, bleak period. Since the Rolling Stones' free fiasco at Altamont, memories of which still lingered, many rock enthusiasts had grown wary, even frightened, of major musical events. In fact, there hadn't been too many. Grand Funk Railroad's performance at Shea Stadium a week earlier could scarcely have been termed musical. The soaring popularity of discordant phenomena such as Grand Funk had been paralleled by an increased trade in cheap heroin outside many rock theaters. The very existence of live music was being threatened. Only a few weeks before, the management of the Fillmore East had decided that its recent audiences had deteriorated far enough. It announced that it was closing its doors forever. "The floor was covered with broken wine bottles some nights," said manager Kip Cohen. "The people coming here were almost Neanderthal in their approach to living."

In short, rock, "smack" and death rapidly were becoming synonymous terms. Not surprisingly, a precarious blend of tension and anticipation swirled around Madison Square Garden until George Harrison stepped onstage to introduce Ravi Shankar. He waited a full minute for the ovation to subside. The crowd heaved a gigantic sigh and sat down to listen patiently to ragas and folk tunes, but throughout the performance and the following disturbing documentary on Bangladesh, the audience continued to bubble with enthusiasm. When the lights dimmed, a tremor shook the Garden. Backstage in the New York Knicks' dressing room, George's team finished sucking their orange slices and prepared to go on.

The first few notes of George's "Wah-Wah" pounded out across a still-darkened hall, then suddenly the spotlights poured onto the most dazzling array of rock musicians ever assembled on the same stage. George had changed from an open-necked shirt and herringbone vest into a white silk suit. Around him were Eric Clapton, Leon Russell, Jesse Davis, Klaus Voormann, Billy Preston, and there at the back, alongside co-drummer Jim Keltner, sat Ringo in a long, black frock-coat. An equally star-studded, nine-voice choir, seven horns and three acoustic guitars completed the orchestra. But George still had one more card to play. Two-thirds of the way through the show, he calmly stepped up to the microphone and announced: "I'd like to introduce my friend Bob." Dylan's surprise appearance drew gasps of amazement.

After five years of abstaining from live performances, two Beatles and their friends had brought the crowds out in thousands. New York had recognized that this was a great occasion, and had treated it accordingly. Allen Klein desperately wanted everything to go well. The ABKCO president had somehow strained an Achilles' tendon during the concert preparations, yet he hobbled around the stagefront with the aid of a cane, tending to even the spotlight details, and yelling orders to seize anyone with a camera. Not until Dylan received a two-minute ovation after his five songs was Klein calm enough to put down his cane and join in the applause.

The performers, their guests and their assistants celebrated afterwards with a party thrown by George's wife,

Pattie, at Jimmy Weston's Tavern. Even reclusive Bob Dylan showed up. He had taken a liking to Klein's radio promotion man, Pete Bennett, a pudgy, rather frightening-looking individual, who supplements his income by writing a "Dis Is Wot's Happening" column for the Gannett newspaper chain. Dylan was highly amused by Bennett and realized his potential as a bodyguard. "Just keep Al Aronowitz away from me," he told him. Bennett obliged, and in return became the only person that evening to have his photograph taken with bashful Bob.

Phil Spector chugged back an inordinate quantity of liquor, sat down at a piano and flailed away at his old hits, "Da-doo-ron-ron," etc. Andy Williams dropped by the tavern, took one quick glance at the riotous proceedings and fled, despite requests from a sozzled Spector for a song. The party lasted until dawn. Unfortunately, reporters were either muzzled or excluded from the celebration, so newspaper accounts of the evening ended with the last note of the concert. But the press was unanimous in its verdict. Delighted with the sophistication, polished performances and glamor of the occasion, *The New York Times,* whose main concern has always been to studiously chronicle the daily chapters of history rather than brighten a subway journey with an exciting story, considered the event sufficiently important to merit a detailed, front-page description. Reviews abounded with superlatives and George received full credit for his handling of the evening. He had been aided by a welcome change in audience reaction to a live Beatle performance. The frenzied screaming which had marred so many Beatle concerts in the sixties was noticeably absent. There was no wild rush to storm the stage, nor any desperate attempt to touch a Beatle. The children, it seemed, had come of age.

Ten tumultuous years had gone by since a Beatle had appeared live without the inevitable, attendant hysteria. Only in the early sixties in Liverpool and Hamburg were the Beatles free from this encumbrance to their music. White silk suits and black frock-coats would have been out of place then. There was no glamor, no polish, no choir and no publicity in the humble surroundings of a Liverpool warehouse district more than a decade ago.

Four boys in black leather jackets and oily jeans had to scramble through a hole in the wall of a dingy cellar onto a makeshift stage, dragging their equipment on after them.

The group's members lacked any trace of sophistication. One was lean and hungry-looking with a long, arrogant nose and slicked-back hair. A real street kid, proud of his tough-guy image. The other guitarists were only slightly less coarse, but more likely to excite teen-age crushes. A good-looking drummer sulked in the background.

Before long, the tough guy would be ready to play.

"Will yer shut yer mouth luv, I'm tryin' ter tune me guitar," he'd yell.

"Yer wot?"

He'd give back an insane grimace and feign fright.

"Geroff the fuckin' stage yer daft bitch." He'd fake a swipe at another advancing teeny with his winkelpicker. The girl would shrink back among her friends. In the meantime, the crowd still filing in at the back—mostly art students in blue jeans—displayed none of the hero worship of the dollies up front. Their interest in these four teddy boys was more detached. It was an incongruous mixture of people passing through the narrow basement entrance, where only an almost invisible chalk mark, "Cavern," gave a clue to the frenzied excitement below ground.

Finally the band was ready. The bass guitarist, whose vocabulary contained the fewest four-letter words, handled the terse announcements.

"That amp turned up?"

"Okay."

"Good golly, Miss Molly. We're gonna have a ball . . ."

The beat went on for three solid hours. Within minutes, perspiration was streaming down the walls and dripping steadily from the ceiling onto the pulsating bodies of several hundred dancers. The flow increased as the night wore on; by midnight the cellar stank. Late in the night, an exhausted crowd filed up the narrow staircase. The boys stripped off their shirts and wrung them out in the narrow street, still littered with piles of rotten fruit and vegetables from warehouse delivery trucks, and the long journey back to the suburbs began.

Liverpool's children are a tough breed of street urchins. They grow up quickly among the uniform rows of grimy nineteenth-century housing, or on the sprawling, suburban council estates. The city's teen-agers of ten years ago had spent most of their childhood playing on piles of debris, bomb sites which still scarred the town in the 1950s, while their parents eked out a living in a depressed seaport. For the frequenters of the Cavern, the "Cave Dwellers" as they came to be known, beat music was one of few available diversions.

The city's working-class Irish population had produced its fair share of hard-core teddy boys in the mid-fifties. They tended to gravitate to the clubs serving the dockland, for the most part small pick-up joints or sailors' haunts, where the juke boxes played American records. The teds saw rock 'n' roll as yet another means of shocking their parents' rigid, working-class values. Drinking, fighting and dancing to loud Bill Haley music in the city's clubs and suburban dance halls became the greasers' absorbing interests. Middle-class parents warned their children "steer clear," but the children were not that easily deterred. Nevertheless, rock 'n' roll in Liverpool at this time was almost exclusively the preserve of working-class youngsters, as indeed it was in the United States.

In the lines outside the Brooklyn Fox in 1954 stood tough-looking hoods with slicked-black D.A. hairstyles. They wore white T-shirts, cigarette packs tucked neatly in the sleeve, rolled-up blue jeans and white socks. Rock 'n' roll's first impresario, Alan Freed, was packing them into his shows. If you were one of the few suburban kids in the line, you kept quiet about your origins. The riotous scenes at the Brooklyn Fox and the Manhattan Paramount left no doubt that rock 'n' roll had come to stay in the United States, but its form was soon to be usurped. It was seized by TV producers, sanitized, watered down and finally wound up packaged on Dick Clark's "American Bandstand," pandering to the weepy romances of Philadelphia's

9

teen-agers. Its guts had been ripped out. It was now wrapped in polyethylene for that great leveler, television.

In England, no B.B.C. producer came forward with the enterprising idea of a rock 'n' roll show. Consequently rock 'n' roll music remained raw and local. The teddy boy era ended and rock 'n' roll began to breach the class barriers, especially in Liverpool where it had a head start. By 1959, there were a dozen beat clubs in the city center, as well as countless suburban dance halls, all being fed by an interminable supply of rock 'n' roll groups competing to play for meager wages. The demand for this music became so heavy that the Cavern ceased to be a jazz club and began to present beat music. One of the first groups to appear there was the Silver Beatles.

Pat Delaney, a fearsome six-foot Irishman with a stubbly beard, had just started to work as the Cavern's bouncer when the club was making its transition, presenting lunchtime beat-music sessions, but exclusively jazz in the evenings.

"This guy turned the corner into Matthew Street. He was wearing a black leather jacket and jeans and was obviously heading for the entrance. I thought: 'Uh, oh, trouble.' "

Pat's beefy arm came down in front of George Harrison.

"We don't allow anyone in 'ere in a leather jacket. Sorry son."

"Well, actually I'm in the band. I'm supposed to be playin' 'ere."

Three teen-age girls quickly came to George's rescue. Reluctantly, Pat raised his arm.

Within a few months, jazz was finally extinguished at the Cavern, and the basement club started to attract a new crowd. The new Cavern audience thought of itself as a rather special clique of mysterious night people. Surprisingly, it never adopted the term "underground." In fact, they were just an ordinary bunch of provincial kids out to irk their parents, who for their part failed to understand why their offspring wanted to spend so many evenings in a dark, damp cellar, from which they'd return with their clothes soaked and ears humming.

The attraction to "beat" soon brought a wide cross-section of Liverpool's children flocking to the new clubs. They ranged from young school kids to art students and poets who hung out at the Crack, a famous Liverpool pub which John Lennon frequented when he was at art school. Slowly they acquired a group consciousness that went beyond the fact that they appreciated the same music. The musicians were close to each other, but more important, the audiences and the musicians were friends. This was five years before the same syndrome of togetherness became evident in San Francisco, another city where groups had an opportunity to develop their music, because they were far removed from any recording studios and the clutches of the record company executives. However, in San Francisco the camaraderie barely survived a single summer, before crass commercialism, hard drugs and several thousand dropouts tore everything apart. In Liverpool it lasted four years and broke up only when a single entrepreneur took the cream of the city's musicians to London. Much of the inevitable hero worship was contained because many of the band members were old school friends of the onlookers. Some of the Liverpool girls may have been idolatrous, but for the most part, the audiences were merely impressed that their friends had matched, and in some cases even surpassed, their American heroes, Presley and Little Richard.

Nobody ever thought to glorify Liverpool as a scene capital as San Franciscans did with their town years later. Liverpool was far too ugly ever to have any pretensions. It had none of the idyllic outdoor trappings that San Francisco could offer. The beat scene in Liverpool was run by the owners of the town's seedy clubs, small-time provincial operators like Alan Williams, who sent the Beatles to Hamburg early in 1960. Williams had already set them up a year earlier with an audition before a London promoter, Larry Parnes, who at the time was handling the big guns in the British pop world, Tommy Steele and Billy Fury. Obviously, Parnes was not too impressed with the Beatles. They were an average hick group. The best he could offer them was a third-rate tour of Scotland, as the back-up group for one of his own acts. The Beatles auditioned at a club called the Blue Angel, a tiny, dark-walled dump in one of the worst areas of central Liverpool, which Williams still owns. On an average night, a dozen or so girls sit around, munching on potato chips and staring at the door, hoping some guys will arrive soon. At the entrance sits a tough-looking bruiser who occasionally gives his back pocket a reassuring pat. Every once in a while he takes out a big wad of notes and counts them furtively. The club's door is kept locked. It is fitted with a peephole and a buzzer system in case of invasions by gangs of rockers. Williams is wise enough to rarely visit his own establishment.

He dislikes the Beatles intensely.

"They let Liverpool down," he says bluntly. "That feller Epstein took them to London along with all the other good groups and that killed the scene here. I held a Liverpool beat group reunion a year or so ago and they were invited, but of course they didn't come. Too bloody big-headed as usual; they always were."

Williams is from the old school of promoters. He offered the Beatles their original fee of fifteen shillings each and all the beer they could drink, if they'd attend his reunion. He's also very proud that it was he who sent them to Hamburg, although at the time he evidently didn't realize the potential value of his exports. Hamburg makes Tijuana look like a playpen. Even though they came from the rough quarters of Liverpool, the Beatles (who at the time numbered five) were initially unnerved by the debauchery of the Reeperbahn and the rest of Hamburg's clubland. Their sleeping quarters turned out to be a cellar, a gents' toilet served as their dressing room and they were told they'd be playing for eight hours a night, seven nights a week. They rose to the challenge.

In retrospect, it was unquestionably the greatest break they ever had, although it didn't seem like it at the time, and it is doubtful whether Alan Williams was considering how much the Beatles' career might benefit from their Hamburg experience when he made the deal. Playing for eight hours at a stretch to a foreign audience, the Beatles were forced to expand their repertoire considerably from the dozen or so songs they knew well enough to play in

Liverpool. More important, they learned the art of performing.

The Germans of Hamburg's clubland expected the group to "Mak Show." They weren't the most sophisticated audience. They called for plenty of action and roared and applauded when John Lennon would scream and curse at them from the stage. Naturally, the Beatles grew in confidence.

"We hated the club owners so much that we jumped about until we broke through the stage," says Lennon. "We'd all end up jumpin' 'round on the floor. Paul'd be doin' 'What I Say' for an hour-an'-a-half. All these gangsters would come in like the Mafia, because they [the clubs] are all run by gangsters. They'd just send a crate of champagne onstage, this sort of imitation German champagne, and we'd have to drink it although it killed us. They'd say, 'Drink it and then do "What I Say."' So we'd have to do this show for them, whatever time of night. If they came in at five in the morning, and we'd been playing for seven hours, they gave us a crate of champagne and we were supposed to carry on. I used to get so pissed, I'd be lyin' on the floor behind the piano, while the rest of the group was playin'. Some shows I went on just in me underpants, and at the Star Club with a toilet seat 'round me neck."

No wonder Hamburg increased their stamina. The experience stood them in good stead later, when they had to cope with an American, a European and a world tour in the same year. But cheap champagne wasn't their only stimulant in the Hamburg clubs. The Germans introduced them to pills. At first, they just took slimming pills to stay awake longer; then they graduated to "black bombers," "purple hearts" and other ups. Ironically, it was another three years before they were to experience the taste of marijuana. Not until 1964 did Bob Dylan offer them their first joint. But the initial barriers to drugs, which any five provincial boys might then be expected to maintain, were broken down in Hamburg. The Beatles' willingness to experiment with anything new they were offered, a behavioral pattern which a generation copied, was evident even then.

13

The intensity of the Beatles' stage performances carried over to their lives outside the clubs. They were brash, vulgar louts with nothing to lose. One particular Sunday morning, Lennon recalls with relish, a group of young nuns was greeted to Hamburg's clubland by the sight of five Beatles, unabashedly relieving themselves in the street outside their club. He claims it was only one of many outrageous incidents. The five proud, young Presleys with their black leather outfits and Brylcreemed hair cared for nothing. They just pounded out their music with an energy which most of the world would never witness in their subsequent, toned-down stage performances. They exuded *machismo*.

Shortly before Christmas 1960, the Beatles straggled back to Liverpool broke and exhausted. They managed to get a booking at Litherland Town Hall, a large suburban Liverpool dance hall, and that night they exploded in front of a stunned audience. The Liverpool teen-agers gaped. Having only seen them previously as an average group at the Cavern lunchtime sessions, they couldn't believe the improvement. For a while they'd been caught up by cute Cliff Richard ballads, yet now this pounding music from these leaping, leather-clad greasers drove them to a frenzy.

The following spring, the five returned to another Hamburg club.

"This time they were wilder than ever," says Astrid Kemp, their photographer friend. She and her boyfriend, Klaus Voormann, were the first avant-garde artists to take an interest in the Beatles.

"I wasn't surprised when they became international stars, because they were all great original talents," says Astrid in her heavily Liverpool-accented English. "I suppose the most important thing I contributed to them was friendship. All that shit people said, that I created their hairstyle, that's rubbish. Lots of German boys had that hairstyle. Stuart had it for a long while and the others copied it." (Stuart Sutcliffe was the Beatle who stayed on in Hamburg with Astrid and died of a brain hemorrhage early the following year.)

"I don't feel anything bad toward them for the breakup," Astrid continued. "They aren't gods and they don't pretend to be. If they have financial problems, why shouldn't they sort them out in court? Nor was I surprised when they broke up, because for such original people, playing together all those years must have become difficult. I haven't seen John or Paul for seven years and if I saw John I wouldn't know what to say to him. He's been through so many changes. George, I saw two years ago. I think he's the most talented now. He was younger than the others and it took him longer to grow up. As for Hamburg now, it's bloody dead. Nothing but boring discotheques; there's no scene here."

The Beatles aren't gods. Astrid Kemp said it. In fact, they were four naïve, provincial boys, three of whom were soon to be extricated from normal growing-up processes. Like other mortals, they were quite capable of meanness and jealousy. This side of their personalities was to be well illustrated the following year, when they ganged up on their drummer, Pete Best, and persuaded their newly acquired manager to fire him. Pete Best was the most popular Beatle. The Cavern girls were strongly attracted to his sulky James Dean image. They even made a habit of sleeping in the garden of his home. Quite simply, the other three Beatles were jealous and insecure.

John, especially, was desperately anxious to get out of Liverpool. Years later, he told Allen Klein that he would have done *anything* to accomplish this. Pat Delaney describes the John Lennon he knew as "sharp as a razor and ambitious as hell," but he could still be provoked into using roughhouse techniques. Although he'd allowed Brian Epstein to put him in a suit, he still resorted to punching his old chum, Bob Wooller, a Cavern disc jockey, for suggesting he was a homosexual.

George, on the other hand, though heavily influenced by John, had not yet become as ambitious. Nor had he developed the hunger for money which dictated so many of his actions in later years. (Some of ABKCO's staff regarded George's decision to do the Bangladesh benefit concert as an amazing reversal of attitude.)

Pat Delaney remembers him coming into the club one

lunchtime and noticing one of the regular girls hanging around the door.

"Yer goin' in?" he asked her.

"Yeah, later on," she told him.

"He slipped me a few shillings," says Pat. " 'Give 'er this and don't tell 'er I gave it to yer,' he told me. I waited until he'd gone, but she guessed what had happened. Tears all over the place."

A few days after this incident, a smooth, impeccably dressed gentleman appeared at the club.

"He was standing at the back, watchin' the boys on-stage," says Pat. "I felt he was embarrassed to be there, he looked so out of place. I went over and said, 'Can I 'elp you sir?'

" 'Er, no thank you,' he said very politely, 'I'm just watching.' "

16

CHAPTER TWO

"Right Then, Brian, Manage Us."

I liked Brian and I had a very close relationship with him for years, like I have with Allen [Klein] because I'm not gonna have some stranger runnin' things, that's all. I like to work with friends. I was the closest with Brian, as close as you can get to somebody who lives a sort of "fag" life, and you don't really know what they're doin' on the side. But in the group, I was closest to him and I did like him.

He had great qualities and he was good fun. He had a flair. He was a theatrical man, rather than a businessman. When he got Cilla Black, his great delight was to dress her and present her. He would have made a great dress designer, 'cause that's what he was made for. With us he was a bit like that. I mean, he literally fuckin' cleaned us up and there were great fights between him and me over me not wanting to dress up. In fact, he and Paul had some kind of collusion to keep me straight because I kept spoilin' the image.

We had complete faith in him when he was runnin' us. To us, he was the expert. I mean originally he had a shop. Anybody who's got a shop must be all right. He went around smarmin' and charmin' everybody. He had hellish tempers and fits and lockouts and y'know he'd vanish for days. He'd come to a crisis every now and then and the whole business would fuckin' stop 'cause he'd be on sleepin' pills for days on end and wouldn't wake up. Or he'd be missin' y'know, beaten up by some docker down the Old Kent Road. But we weren't too aware of it. It was later on we started findin' out about those things.

We'd never have made it without him and vice versa. Brian contributed as much as us in the early days, although we were the talent and he was the hustler. He wasn't strong enough to overbear us. Brian could never make us do what we really didn't want to do.

John Lennon.
August 1971.

Pop music's managers in the 1950s were not noted for their concern to prolong and advance artists' careers.* When an artist or group was hot, most managers grabbed as many beans as possible and fled. They didn't give a damn if the public was fleeced and cared even less about servicing their clients. The less financially secure musicians were kept, the harder they worked. In most cases, a manager was a hard-nosed manipulator, whose main concern was with percentages. Pop musicians by the thousands had piled up on the scrap-heap.

Brian Epstein profoundly altered this state of affairs.

---

* Colonel Tom Parker, Presley's protective shield, was a notable exception.

His management of the Beatles was nothing less than a total emotional commitment. During his short career, he brought quality, style and vision to a business which had been sadly lacking in all of these elements. Many successful managers today admit they learned a lot by following his example closely. Others have attacked him as a bad businessman, a gambler and a dilettante. When he died in 1967, the narrow-hearted British public gloated that it was possible for a man to be so rich and successful, and yet unhappy. It was almost a relief for them to discover that Epstein was vulnerable to common, trivial anxieties. His name was quickly forgotten. Nobody seemed to associate his passing with the increased turbulence of the Beatles' career.

As manager of an unprecedented show-business phenomenon, Epstein's origins were the most unlikely. He was the elder son of comfortably affluent Jewish parents who owned a furniture-and-record store in Liverpool. After a string of unhappy failures at several of England's notorious private schools, where as a frail and sensitive boy he was continually teased and bullied, Brian began work as a salesman in the family furniture store. Although successful at his new metier, he demonstrated an even greater talent for design and presentation, exercising the exquisite taste which he displayed throughout his life. This was certainly due in part to the influence of his mother, Queenie, a very elegant and refined lady, who encouraged her son to follow her example. "I was, and still am very interested in the way things should be displayed and I have a self-devouring passion for quality," Epstein declared in his autobiography.* His excellent taste was not merely confined to furniture. He went on to apply his artistic discrimination on another level, presenting four talented but unpolished musicians in a manner which made them appealing to as wide a cross-section of the public as possible, just as he had done with the chairs in his father's furniture store.

At eighteen, Epstein was drafted into the army, but after a year's service was discharged as mentally and emo-

* *A Cellarful of Noise,* Souvenir Press.

tionally unsuited to military service. He went back to work for his father in the record department of the store. His enthusiasm for the job was short-lived. Within a few months, he decided to go against his father's wishes and pursue a career in theater, an interest he had nurtured since he had acted in his school plays. Somehow, he obtained a place at London's Royal Academy of Dramatic Art, the finest drama school in Britain, but he quickly grew to hate actors and all the social trappings that went with an acting career. Before long, he was back in Liverpool again, where his persevering father persuaded him to take charge of the record division in a new store. Disillusioned with his own initiatives, he decided to treat the work more seriously.

From its opening the new business was successful. Brian devised an inventory system which ensured that records were replaced before they went out of stock. It was a simple yet ingenious technique, and the first manifestation of another managerial quality which later impressed all who did business with him—his astonishing ability to attend to all manner of detail, no matter how minor. Five years later, this same regard for detail ensured that the Beatles bowed at the end of their appearance on the Ed Sullivan show, a gesture which won over the hearts of seventy million Americans.

In 1959, yet another branch of the Epstein family record business (North End Music Stores) was opened in the city's main shopping center and Brian was placed in charge. Within two years, he could boast that the store offered the finest record selections in the North of England. He was shrewd enough to advertise in the new, local pop music newspaper, *Merseybeat,* and he even began to review records for its columns. It was his first contact, however slight, with rock 'n' roll. A few months later in November 1961, the now well-known incident occurred in his store. A young man asked for a record called "My Bonnie" by the Beatles and Epstein had never heard of it. As was his policy, he spared no efforts to locate the disc, which had been recorded in Germany a year earlier, and he soon discovered that the Beatles were a Liverpool group, playing regularly in a nearby club. The elegant record store owner decided to visit the Cavern.

At this time he was twenty-seven years old. His life to this point had been at best unexciting, more often disappointing. A number of affairs had ended unhappily for him and one romance with a girl working at his store fizzled out soon after his Cavern visit. Although he confided to friends that he felt doomed to be a middle-aged businessman, he was desperately seeking an outlet for his creative talents, recognizing that in his present position he was operating well below capacity. Brian Epstein was not the stuffed shirt that many people supposed him to be. He was attracted to many other aspects of life. The dingy cellar entranced him, as did the four leaping figures in leather jackets onstage. Some years later, he explained his true feelings about the famous encounter to his American attorney, Nat Weiss, with whom he became close friends and eventually a business partner.

"Brian loved all sorts of slimy, seedy scenes," says Weiss. "I used to bring him to the Peppermint Lounge on Forty-fifth Street near my office and he enjoyed the place immensely. He adored checking out the truck driver hang-outs and other such places on the block. It was exactly for this reason that he was so fascinated with the Cavern and the Beatles."

Whether he was fascinated with the Beatles or not, Epstein decided to smarten them up a bit. He stopped them smoking, swearing and eating sandwiches onstage and insisted they look clean and wear suits for performances. John Lennon later criticized Brian for "putting us in suits." Such a rash statement only indicates his own unwillingness to understand some of the reasons for the Beatles' universal acclaim. Brian cut down the length of their performances and encouraged them to play only the best of their repertoire, instead of a new batch of songs each time. Gradually he booked them into bigger and better ballrooms, then into theaters and finally concert halls. He also succeeded, after many disappointments, in securing them a recording contract with E.M.I. As he once told an American reporter shortly after Beatlemania hit the United States: "One did everything. One worked very hard. One shouted from the rooftops about this group when there was no enthusiasm for groups. People thought you were mad, but you went on shouting."

From the moment Epstein signed the Beatles, he insisted that other business people show them respect. Although they were earning only thirty-five dollars a night in local dance halls, he treated them as if they were worth $100,000 a booking. The local club and dance hall owners had to do the same, or they didn't get the group. Epstein certainly never lacked confidence in his protégés. On the day they placed their names on his contract, he told his parents they would become the greatest entertainers ever and a worldwide cult.

"Brian used to theorize that if you surrounded people with success, or at least made them feel that they were en route to success, then the growth in their own confidence simply enhanced the process," says his former personal assistant, Wendy Moger.

Brian Epstein entered the pop music jungle as a talented businessman on a provincial city level. He was not a Midas touch genius, but other more fundamental, interpersonal qualities compensated for this particular deficiency and accounted for his overall managerial expertise. "In fact, he learned a lot about business from managing the Beatles," says Tony Barrow, former press officer of Epstein's company, Nems Enterprises.

Barrow recalls that TV executives would call Brian and make him an offer for a show featuring the Beatles. Brian wouldn't know whether to accept the offer or not. He would blithely say, "Call you back tomorrow," because he wanted time to consult his business advisers. So even though the TV people were offering a lot of money, they reasoned among themselves that it wasn't enough. The next morning before Brian could get back to them, a message would be on his desk. The bewildered TV executives had doubled their offer.

What Epstein lacked in business finesse was made up for by his tremendous energy. He would arrive back in London at six in the morning after an eleven-hour flight from Los Angeles, and with no wife and family to return to, he went straight to his office. Barrow frequently got calls from him at such inconvenient times. Endless hours were devoted to the careers of his ever-growing, surrogate family—the fortunate beat groups he had elevated from the Liverpool clubs. While the Beatles and his other groups played, he arranged their next tours. When he met Presley's manager, Colonel Tom Parker, the stony-faced southerner was amazed that Brian could cope with it all. "I have only Elvis and he takes up all my time. How do you do it?" Parker demanded. Epstein just brushed away the question with a haughty laugh.

As the fastest rising star in the British pop business, the Beatles' manager naturally aroused the envy of the established London show-business families. Many of them hated him, but were forced to concede that he had initiative and ability. They realized he wasn't just a fast-talking, provincial boy who stuck a cigar between gritted teeth whenever he came to the big city. His natural elegance and grace enabled him to move with ease among the cream of London show business. Nor was the British capital the limit of his horizon. Although he was bubbling when his most successful group so distinguished themselves at the 1963 Royal Variety performance, a charity debacle staged before the Royal Family, he already had laid more ambitious plans for them.

Earlier that year he had scouted the American record companies and impresarios, but had met with a frosty reception. After all, nothing important in pop music had ever come out of England. How far did this snappily dressed limey think he was going to go with his Beatles? Epstein was undeterred. He knew his product was perfectly tailored for the American market; all it required was exposure. It took a terrific fight with Ed Sullivan before he obtained top billing for the Beatles on the TV host's show. Then, he returned to England, confident that success was assured. In January 1964, his eye for presentation proved correct.

With the devastating success of the "mop tops" in the United States, the Beatle retinue snowballed, as did the staff of Brian's company, Nems. Although Epstein insisted on competence, he liked to surround himself with people who were at the same time amusing. His entourage included a healthy contingent of characters. Among them was Derek Taylor, who became Brian's personal assistant shortly after the Beatles' first American tour. Their working relationship was not the most equable and terminated in high drama. Taylor borrowed his boss's limousine to entertain a new lady friend and Brian was left stranded outside a Manhattan theater. After a huge row, Taylor left for Los Angeles, where he wound up doing publicity for the Byrds and later took an important hand in organizing the Monterey Pop Festival. His Sunset Strip office, cool English arrogance and utter disdain for the plastic city made him something of a legend with the L.A. chickie babes, but his natural eloquence and David Niven looks made him a much-sought-after public-relations man. He now works in that capacity for Warner Brothers Records in London. In his tapered shirt, bell-bottom trousers and bright red socks, he sits alongside a beautiful, if unskilled, blonde secretary who stares at him adoringly, as indeed he occasionally does at her.

The ruckus over the limousine did not breach his relationship with his former boss. They were soon firm friends and Taylor still retains a deep affection for the Beatles' manager.

"Brian was a terrible autocrat and if anything went wrong he could be a shit," says Taylor, with the benefit of his experience. "At the same time he could be very generous. I ghost-wrote his autobiography *A Cellarful of Noise* before we temporarily fell out. He offered me a thousand pounds and a two and a half percent royalty. When we met later in Los Angeles, he said, 'I think I shortchanged you on the book.' He whipped out his checkbook and wrote me another check for the same amount.

"Eppy was impeccable as the Beatles' manager. His devotion to them was total and he gave his life for them. He had great intelligence and instinct as a business manager, and although I was some years older than him, I recognized his maturity and skill in judgment. He understood the Beatles completely and he enabled them to flower as Beatles. He tidied them up, put them into a uniform like the military, smoothed out the wrinkles and taught them how to bow.

"His relationship with them was highly personal. They were able to bully him a bit because he was like a father figure to them. This parental exercise finally became too much for him, even though he had a competent staff of lawyers and accountants. He was literally drained by the efforts required of him. He wasn't a truly international playboy, as some people thought. He liked to cultivate the image of a jet-setter, but I knew him better. He had a lot of strength and he took a lot of shit."

Epstein was a lonely bachelor, who always needed company and reassurance. Brian Sommerville had filled the role before he was replaced by Derek Taylor. Later, Brian brought into his organization his close friends from Liverpool, Geoffrey Ellis and Peter Brown. Wendy Moger, a tall, willowy English blonde with the degree of refinement Brian Epstein would demand, became his personal assistant after Taylor left. Wendy was the only woman ever to loom large at Nems. She was close friends with the Italian filmmakers, Fellini, Visconti and Zeffirelli. Brian was very impressed and wanted to meet them all.

"I was corralled into doing all this madness," said Wendy. "I first met them all in New York where I had been working for a record company. I walked into the Plaza to find an immensely cool Brian sitting behind a huge breakfast table. 'Ah, do come in, my dear,' he said, 'would you like some tea?'

"Pop music was Brian's entire life at this time. He used to say his idea of heaven was to have ten hits in a row on the charts. He was very close to all the Beatles and really doted on them. He took particular delight in showing them old film clips of themselves. He was very amused about one of Ringo saying if he ever became really famous, he would leave and open a chain of hairdressing salons.

"My favorite memory of Brian was when the boys were in Nassau filming *Help*. We all hated Nassau, and as the boys were busy, he and I decided to go to New York for the weekend. As usual, Brian made us late for the plane and the Pan American staff refused to help us weigh in our baggage. Brian was furious. He sat down on

the plane and immediately composed an angry letter saying, 'The Beatles and Brian Epstein will never fly Pan
American again.' He handed it to a steward just before
the plane took off. When we landed at Kennedy Airport,
there were at least twenty Pan Am officials bowing and
scraping and doing their best to apologize. Brian withdrew
his threat, adding that he hoped all would go well on the
journey back.

"But on Sunday morning, with the plane due to leave
at 10:00 A.M., he refused to get up. It was inevitable that
we were going to be late for the plane, as of course we
were. He deliberately took his time and poor Pan Am
were doing their best to be accommodating. When we
got to the airport, they'd held up the plane, reserved front
seats for us in first class, and they even threw our baggage
into the compartment after us. Brian took his seat lei-
surely as the plane moved down the runway, glanced at
his Jacques Cartier wristwatch and said very loudly,
'Hmmm, I see we're seven minutes late taking off.' I was
hysterical. You had to love him. He was such an arrogant
bastard, but so cool.

"He was very difficult to work for. My first mistake was
when I got the Beatles to sign some minor contract detail
for an American radio executive. Brian was out at the
time, so I got the boys together and they signed. When
he came back I told him what had happened. He went
ghostly white. 'They've never signed anything in their
lives before,' he said, stunned. He was immensely protective of them and I don't think they ever realized how
much he was doing. Paul said something once that sticks
in my mind because it was about Allen Klein, who Paul
now hates, of course. Brian had gone to America to sort
out the row that was raging there, because John Lennon
supposedly had said that the Beatles were more popular
than Jesus Christ. Evidently, Paul didn't think Brian was
doing a good job because he said, 'If he [Brian] was Allen
Klein, he'd just have his photo taken shaking Billy
Graham's hand.' "

It was an ironic and ungrateful remark by Paul Mc-
Cartney, to say the least. Brian had been ill at the time

and was on vacation in Wales. Still, there may have been some justification for Paul's feeling critical toward him.

Brian had always dressed impeccably, lived elegantly and surrounded himself with the very best of everything, but he never took things easy. Although he socialized more now than he ever had previously, he still devoted a vast amount of time to his work. It was his energy level which was beginning to decline. The Jesus Christ incident occurred in the summer of 1966. At this time, the effects of prolonged, heavy drug use were starting to tell on Epstein. Even so, he still insisted on protecting the Beatles and struggled against his own incapacities to try and attend to every detail of their career, as he had always done.

Wendy Moger remembers his deterioration as sudden and tragic. She recounts one incident from an evening she spent with Brian at this time in a London bar.

"I leaned across the counter to take a handful of peanuts, when he grabbed my arm and said, 'What the hell do you think you're doing?' I said, 'Eating peanuts.' He let go of my arm, very embarrassed. 'Oh,' he said, 'I thought they were pills.' "

Brian Epstein had reached a crucial stage in his brief and tumultuous pop career. By the end of 1966 his drug problem was acute. He was using drugs to escape from the increasing pressures of running Nems. For a while he refused to relinquish the reins, but in January 1967, he brought in Robert Stigwood, an Australian with some show-business experience, as co-managing director, and turned the day-to-day management of the company over to him. He felt that attending to the Beatles would prove enough for his diminished energies. Many of his other artists felt they were being shortchanged because he wasn't paying attention to them. He was extremely upset when he learned of their feelings, but was powerless to do much to compensate. The monster he'd created was out of control.

At the same time, he was unhappy because the Beatles' tours had ended. He didn't quite know what to do with himself or them. They began to work on "Sergeant Pepper" and he saw less and less of them socially. His close friend and business associate, Geoffrey Ellis, recalls that Brian had adored the tours because he felt like the fifth Beatle when the show was on the road. He began to lose some of his previously astute business judgment. His decision to put on rock concerts at London's Saville Theater cost him a lot of money. Profits, however, were not the main motivations behind this venture. He wanted to act as a producer, a function he regarded as a substitute for his failure to realize an acting career. He felt he wanted to grow, as the Beatles had grown.

Brian grew increasingly nervous as his contract with the group was due to expire. "He was hesitant to discuss either them or the contract," says his brother, Clive. "I got the impression that the outcome of the contract renewal would have been reduced terms for Brian."

Although it seems unlikely that any of the Beatles wanted to leave Epstein, they were certainly less tightly knit now that the touring had ended. The children were also beginning to quarrel more amongst themselves. Personality differences surfaced as they grew up. With their increasing self-assurance, they clung to their father less.

"You have to realize what a superhuman job Brian did just keeping them together," says the producer of their first American concerts, Sid Bernstein. "How did he do it? . . . He was just a great diplomat, a psychiatrist without a diploma, who sat on dynamite, arguments, everything, because even then they often had four different points of view. They were also exposed to more pressures than any other band ever or since. The moment Brian died, the inevitable happened. They've never worked a date together since. Brian was never a sociable person; he was very cool and aloof, but as far as they were concerned he was big brother."

As a businessman, Brian Epstein was a vivid contrast in 1967 to the man who, a few years earlier, had employed all his gall and confidence in his battle with Ed Sullivan. Although he had never been magnanimous in his business negotiations, he always insisted that his deals were fair to all parties. "I am neither greedy nor hard, but I am deeply concerned in preserving the status and upward climb of artists. This is what they pay me twenty-five percent for," read his autobiography.* Now he cared very little about business; in the months before his death he gave it less and less of his attention. His affairs became tangled. Many of the attacks on his business ability are based on his conduct during these final months.

"Allen Klein has called Brian a bad businessman because he says he's made more money for the Beatles in a shorter time than Brian did," says Sid Bernstein. "But, by a bad businessman, do you mean that you don't get every dollar you can seize? Does a bad businessman mean you have some humanity for the other guy's feelings? Brian did. I studied his style and approaches and I found them admirable. He did the best he possibly could for his artists. He was dealing in very high stakes and this placed a great strain on him. The ball game was far different than any of us know. To cope with that, you had to be far stronger than he was."

Brian alienated several of his friends and employees in the last few months of his life. With his heavy intake of drugs he became moody and peevish and easily lost his temper. But occasionally the underlying charm still showed through.

"He could be an absolute bastard," says Geoffrey Ellis. "The longer I stayed at Nems, the less friendly I became with him, because of his monstrousness towards his staff. But only a few weeks before he died, I went with some friends to an opera at Glyndebourne, a few miles from where Brian was staying at his country house. He insisted on treating myself and my guests to a splendid picnic spread. He went to great trouble to arrange it all himself. He could be incredibly generous."

In the last few years of Brian's life, his New York attorney, Nat Weiss, became his closest friend. Weiss was one of New York's successful divorce attorneys when he first met Brian in 1964. Since then, he has become an equally successful musicians' attorney and promoter, representing James Taylor, Cat Stevens, Miles Davis, Peter Asher and John McLaughlin. He has also maintained some contact with the Beatles, although, since Brian's death, he

* *A Cellarful of Noise,* Souvenir Press.

has in no way been involved in the saga of their business affairs.

"I've been successful only because my initial exposure to the music business was through Brian Epstein," says Weiss. "I was very fortunate. His standards still prevail with me. The sad thing is that I've never met anyone in the pop business with his class, integrity and charisma."

Weiss had had only superficial contact with the pop world before he met Epstein. He had represented another English manager, Larry Parnes, in the early sixties. Parnes had brought Tommy Steele to the United States, where like most other British pop musicians before the Beatles, he proved not too successful on the American charts. When Epstein left for the States with the Beatles, Parnes advised him to look up Weiss. As things turned out, the two were introduced at a party, but Brian remembered the name. Within a few weeks he was looking for an attorney and asked Weiss to handle certain matters for him. As a result of their meetings, the two became close friends.

They began to see a lot more of each other. Weiss made a habit of meeting Brian at the airport whenever he came to New York. When the Beatles played Shea Stadium in August 1965, he stayed at Weiss's house over the weekend because he was being plagued with telephone calls at the Waldorf Astoria Hotel. Before he left for California the next day with the Beatles, to meet Colonel Tom Parker and Elvis Presley, he asked Weiss if he'd like to be involved in artist-management. The New York attorney told him he would.

Soon afterward, Weiss found a group playing in a bar in Atlantic City. Epstein advised him to work with them and offered to help him the next time he came to New York.

"When he returned, I'd found them work in a discotheque in Greenwich Village," says Weiss. "Brian changed their name from 'The Rondells' to 'The Cyrkle' and I signed them to Columbia Records. They made some acetates and I sent them to Brian. He phoned me and said, 'I know that record "Red Rubber Ball" will sell a million copies.' It did.

"It was then he asked me to become his partner. We

set up a company called Nemperor Artists and The Cyrkle was placed on the Beatles' 1966 tour. We had a very close association and worked continually together until he died. Brian taught me a great deal about management, and even more about promotion. He had a sense of promotion such as I've never seen duplicated in my lifetime. I think he was a rare genius.

"Brian's commitment to the Beatles was a very emotional one. He sought more than a business or an investment involvement with them. It was almost a personal crusade with him. He virtually devoted his life to their welfare and success. I don't think they realized until long afterward how he absorbed all the shocks. so that the hassles and problems never reached them. He was very dedicated to every one of them, personally and collectively. His concern was that they should be shielded from anything unpleasant, or unfavorable, that might detract from their concentration or their artistic success. He thoroughly insulated them from any business involvement whatsoever, recognizing that they were artists and not businessmen, a fact that proved to be more true than he probably ever imagined later on. It's true that he was not as money-hungry as subsequent people have been with respect to them, but he preserved them and made them grow. His mystique grew too, because he was the only person who ever matched them as a personality.

"When they were attacked, he was the one who suffered. I saw that happen often. When the John Lennon-Jesus Christ incident occurred, I phoned Brian because the Beatles were about to do an American tour and I thought Brian should know that their records were being burned in the Bible Belt. He came to the States and a flurry of reporters met him at the airport. We got into the limousine and the first question he asked was, 'What will it cost to cancel the tour?' I said, 'A million dollars.' He said, 'I'll pay it. I'll pay it out of my own money. I don't want anything to happen to them. I'm not going to subject them to any abuse because if anything happens to any one of them, I'll never forgive myself.'

"The Beatles all related very well to Brian and he had immense insight into each one of them. They were four

31

such distinct personalities and Brian treated them all differently. He really didn't have any favorites. Once, he sat up all night in Cleveland on a tour and gave me his précis into each one of them. He said that Ringo, while the least creative, had no hangups about not being the equal of John and Paul, and that's why he was so good in the group. George, he felt, was the most insecure and paranoid about money. He was very devoted to John and developed a very fatherly feeling toward him. He got much closer to Paul in the year before he died. Certainly, Brian was a homosexual. In fact, I'm convinced that this was the strongest single reason for him wanting to manage the Beatles in the first place. He was very attracted to John when he first met him. Brian was the only person I ever saw dominate John Lennon. When he wanted to be cold, he was icy. There was nothing colder than a cold Brian Epstein.

"But Brian was hurt if they felt hurt about something. He would shield them to the point that he wouldn't permit anyone to speak in front of them about anything that might tend to upset them. You could never talk about them unless he initiated the conversation, which he very rarely did. He could be drunk or stoned and he would never mention them, and if anybody did, he would just ignore the comment or refuse to pursue the conversation. But if somebody said something inaccurate about them, with his usual eye for detail he would immediately correct them but would add nothing more. His reserve on the subject was incredible.

"Brian was quite prepared to put himself on the line for them. He would have died for them, as he quite possibly did. When Paul McCartney announced to the world that he took LSD, Brian volunteered the fact that he'd taken it too, only to show Paul that he was with him. Actually, Brian was taking LSD way before any of the Beatles took it. I can remember them all questioning Brian about his experiences with it, asking him what it was like. It was he who was way ahead of his time in this respect."

Although Epstein had acquired a fondness for drugs since his initiation into the pop scene, during the last year of his life he stepped up his dosages of pills. On many occasions, it was a struggle for him to function. Weiss recalls bringing him around from a heavy dose of Seconals in the spring of 1967, a few months before his death, and managing to get him to the WOR radio station in time to do an interview with Murray the K. Weiss kept the tape of the show. Despite Brian's physical condition, he was amazingly lucid and eloquent, a marked contrast to the babbling AM disc jockey.

Shortly after this interview, Brian became extremely paranoid as a result of his heavy use of drugs. Weiss says he was worried about the "Sergeant Pepper" album because Paul McCartney was insisting that this was a great work of art and therefore all the people the Beatles liked should be on the cover.

"Before he left for London, he became convinced that his plane was going to crash and he would be killed," says Weiss. "He wrote a note on a scrap of paper and gave it to me shortly before takeoff. It read: 'Brown Paper Jackets for Sgt. Pepper's Lonely Hearts Club Band (album).'

"A few months later he died, and all the people associated with Nems, his friends whom he'd brought from nowhere, all thought they could manage the Beatles. Of course, the Beatles thought they could manage themselves. Well, they certainly proved themselves wrong. There was a chemistry in that group of five. The right people coagulated at the right time and Brian was irreplaceable. My disappointment came when the Beatles rejected all the things that were so great about Brian. They said we don't want an inspirational, sensitive manager who is competent with respect to our business dealings. We don't want to build a music scene beyond ourselves. We want to 'zap' everybody. It was like a vengeance to get back at people. They took delight in getting rid of a lot of people, some of whom I admit should have been gotten rid of, but they did it in the wrong way. They were cold and crass with people who'd worked with them for a long time, and some of the people behaved very cowardly toward them.

"In May 1969, three of them retained Allen Klein to handle their business affairs and Paul, of course, wouldn't go along with this. He wanted his in-laws, the Eastmans, to run things. Klein had said some years earlier that one day he would have the Beatles. He came to power by denouncing Brian Epstein. Brian actually met him once in America. He refused to shake his hand. Brian was usually very cordial.

"Klein saw that here was a gold mine available for further tapping. His technique was to say, 'Oh, everybody in the world's been cheating you.' Lennon, of course, was already very much interested in, and influenced by, Yoko Ono at this time, and Yoko, who was really more concerned about the movie deals Allen Klein was going to make her, saw an enormous opportunity to have her films *Two Virgins* and *Smile* put in the same category as *Gone with the Wind*. So Klein had the greatest vehicle for breaking in Lennon, and George, who I think was most keen to engage anybody who would protect his finances, or would tell him he was being cheated, went along. Both of them believed the things Klein said.

"You can't really admire this Talleyrand type of existence with people, but there is a poetic justice in this world and it's all coming home to roost. Klein may have made them more money, but the thing that probably meant more to him than anything was his ego. He never produced a performing Beatles. He never managed to unite them. In the end, he provoked an atmosphere of distrust about their finances and he effectively brought to an end the era of the Beatles. Paul, as a single artist, has failed to measure up to the expectations people had of him. With regard to Brian, I suspect Paul's the most sensitive. At least he's never put him down.

"For me, the most disappointing one is John. I think his conduct in turning his back on the past altogether is disgraceful. He's become a very selfish person. I mean, when I think of how Brian was so dedicated to John, and how John has said that he's not interested in anything else but money, and he doesn't care at whose expense he gets it, nor who gets hurt in the pursuit of it, I think it's the most hypocritical thing I've ever heard. I remember John saying just before Brian's funeral, 'We will continue to do things in Brian's memory.'

34

"George's last thoughtful gesture was to give me a sunflower to throw into Brian's grave. Since then, he's wanted a tough businessman to run things. George has done some fine things, but he's most interested in what happens to the money he earns. I respect an artist for wanting to be properly compensated for what he does, but if the standard is who's going to make the most money for me, and I don't care how unfair the deal is, then I'm sorry for him. George says, 'I wish we'd had Allen Klein all those years.' I venture to say if they'd had Allen Klein all those years, they'd still be playing at the Cavern in Liverpool. The boys are now in the hands of the money men. They're not happening and I think they were finished as Beatles the day Brian died. I don't think the Beatles would have happened at all if Brian had been motivated exclusively by money.

"That's not to say that Brian was a bad businessman. Brian considered not only the money involved, but the total effect of what he was doing. Everything has to be evaluated in the context of its own time. The music publishing and personal appearance deals which he made were not what they would be today because the market was very different then. It has grown from year to year. Brian had a compulsion that a deal should be fair so that it would work. It was never his intention to do a deal in order to take advantage of the other side. It's true his deals could have been better, but they would have been unfair because they would have been overreaching.

"The recording contract he got them with E.M.I. was as good a contract as any for a new group by the standards of the time. It's easy to say now that it was not as good as it should have been; today a third-rate group is going to get the kind of deal the Beatles got in 1963. For the time, it was certainly good because much attention was paid to their artistic freedom, which Brian considered so important. There was a time when it was thought that the Beatles were a fleeting phenomenon which would not survive. I know for a fact that prior to the release of the 'Revolver' album, Columbia Records thought that the Beatles had peaked and had had it. But Brian always treated them as if they were going to survive forever.

"He was a very honest man. He's criticized for the fact that he never got involved in any way-out tax schemes. He was approached many times with respect to tax schemes which might be considered a bit shady, but Brian didn't want any stigma either for himself or for them. When the Beatles' music publishing company, Northern Songs, went public, the Beatles received stock in that company. Frankly, the bulk of John's and Paul's assets in 1969 was probably the result of the sale of that stock which Brian placed in their hands. Klein told them to sell it of course, which is not any great managerial feat, to say to somebody sell your stock, and then say I've made you ten million dollars, as Klein did. It's like saying to someone sell your building. Most of the deals that I'm aware of that Allen Klein has made are not so special or spectacular, except for the E.M.I. deal which is an excellent contract. I think any competent lawyer could have made the same deals for a lot less charge against the Beatles. It's true Brian was not basically a finance man, but he had good sense about money and would listen to people before making up his own mind."

Only in the last six months of his life did Epstein abandon his interest in money. He wanted to get away from the details of running a business, to try and prove that he wasn't just limited to one field. As the Beatles began to try and prove themselves in other ways, so Brian looked for a way of fulfilling himself.

"The Beatles weren't a substitute fame for Brian," says Weiss. "He was very much a person in his own right. A lot of people said he was a frustrated actor, who'd found his fame through somebody else. I don't think that's fair. He had ambitions and desires of his own and this showed shortly before he died. He opened that Saville Theater in London at great financial loss, not only because he wanted to produce shows, but because he felt he had an obligation to bring American groups to England.

"Brian was the most influential man in pop music in the 1960s. He almost singlehandedly generated the power to revolutionize an age. He was a pioneer who was paving the way. Nobody played stadiums before the Beatles. There was no frame of reference for him; he was laying the foundations. He had the ability to get to the core of a problem and understand what was important. He was a visionary almost to the point that it was frightening. I was shocked by his element of clairvoyance because he'd say, 'This is going to happen. If you do this, I guarantee that will happen.' Very often, your own sense of logic would tell you he was wrong, but almost invariably he was right. He would go into these withdrawn stares, predicting things that would very often happen. Toward the end, he was telling me he would not live to see the things he was predicting.

"It's sad that he's not remembered for the virtues which he epitomized. Honesty, fairness and integrity were his very nature and it was unfortunate that the press failed to recognize his class and sophistication. Brian could walk into a room in his underwear and you could tell he had class and was important, even if you didn't know he was the Beatles' manager. He even conducted his homosexuality with integrity. I remember once in California he was held up at gunpoint by a musician boyfriend, who got away with a case full of money. Brian refused to pursue the matter and press charges. Perhaps the greatest error of judgment about Brian was made at his own funeral. It was held in a little Jewish cemetery near Liverpool and the rabbi said, 'Brian Epstein was the symbol and victim of the malaise of his generation.' Yes, he actually said that."

Epstein was confined to nursing homes for several weeks during the last year of his life. He confided to Nat Weiss that he felt control of Nems was slipping from his hands and that money was being spent far too easily. Three months before he died, he even asked the New York attorney to become his manager, as well as his partner in Nemperor Artists. Weiss agreed to do this.

Brian had been exhausted by the efforts required to run Nems, oversee his other diverse investments and act as a parent to the Beatles. A London stockbroker, who met him a few weeks before his death, said he'd never seen a more haggard and worn-looking man in his life. He felt Epstein had been trying desperately to see to every detail of the lives of four successful people, which he considered worthy of his attention, whereas this range of responsibilities would normally be delegated among many branches of an entire organization.

Epstein was prone to burdening himself with more responsibilities than he could well manage. Northern Songs was a public company and he had to account for the Beatles' behavior to the financiers, who for the most part regarded the Beatles as four wild-ass kids, earning far more money than they should have been. He was also responsible for his own considerable pride, which could only be maintained if he was successful with the Beatles' public image. His recognition of these responsibilities, and the need to relinquish some of them, was expressed in a letter written to Nat Weiss a month before he died.

"The boys've gone to Greece to buy an island," he wrote. "I think it's a dotty idea but they're no longer children and must have their own sweet way. A few weeks ago they all came to Sussex for a weekend. Mick and Marianne joined us on the Sunday. Poor Mick, I hope he gets off when the appeal comes up at the end of the month. Of course, the whole thing from the beginning was stupidly handled. . . ."

Brian Epstein's last letter to Nat Weiss was written on August 23rd, 1967, four days before he died. It was used by a Westminster coroner to establish that the cause of his death was an accidental overdose of drugs. It read as follows:

Dear Nat: Just got your letter of the 21st. We have since talked on the telephone when I told you that Sunday and Monday I'd quite like to take a yacht trip on similar lines to those which we did last year, when I came to the States in connection with Jesus Christ. Maybe on the Sunday we could have all manner of lovely, pretty mortal persons aboard and then on Monday we could mix the company a bit with the likes of Eric Anderson, etc., Bobby Colomby, The Cyrkle and other celebrated beautiful people. Actually I'll leave all this in your hands because provided I don't have to stay at a place other than the

Towers, I'm sure I'll enjoy whatever entertainment you provide or arrange.

Incidentally, I hear from Geoffrey that my dear old friend, Brian Bedford, is appearing in something with Peter Ustinov at the Lincoln Center—could you arrange for us to see it while I'm in N.Y.? Apart from that I'm not aware of anything else to see at the theatre—are you? Maybe it might be fun to see Judy Garland one night (if tickets are difficult try her or her people directly—I do know her).

Assuming that the Royal York is the very top in Toronto I'll be happy. I don't think it's the same hotel I've stayed at on my two previous visits to Toronto with the Beatles. But then I don't remember its name and it was huge, not very good. When you requested Jarvis to arrange the accommodation I trust you asked him to include reservations for yourself.

Hope that we've got a lovely place in L.A. to stay in, so that we can entertain all the beautiful people suitably, and I hope you managed to confer with Derek.

I also hope that I'm not asking for too many things. But I'm anxious for this to be a good trip for us both. Anyway (say I indignantly) you are my manager.

Eric's album makes lovely, happy, contented dreamy listening. I'm very addicted to Anderson.

> Til the 2nd.
> love, flowers, bells,
> be happy and look forward
> to the future
> with love
> Brian.

CHAPTER THREE

The Epstein Formula Leads to Beatlemania

The Beatles placed their signatures on Epstein's contract in January 1962. From that moment Brian took care of everything. They became emancipated souls. While he scurried about attending to mundane chores, they were free to float to those misty realms where an artist's talent can flourish, unhampered by time-consuming, quotidian anxieties. Their futures lay far from the grimy, working-class Liverpool tenements. Paul McCartney was spared the drudgery of an inglorious career as a trucking firm's delivery boy, an occupation he had pursued for a while after the group returned from Hamburg.

Four naïve, sloppy boys sat uncomfortably in the office of this well-spoken, dignified gentleman. They were unnerved by the prospect of being managed. Three years of playing for subsistence wages in some of Europe's most dilapidated dives, being manipulated by a string of unscrupulous shysters, had made them wary of any such offers. Yet, there was something in the carriage of this paragon of gentility which appealed to their aspirations. Their decision was instant.

"Right then, Brian. Manage us, now. Where's the contract? I'll sign it," said Lennon.

Epstein said he never knew what prompted him to ask this group of boys to come to his office for a meeting. For so timid an individual, whose future then seemed inexorably linked to the vested interests of his family, it was a bizarre tangent; more a personal than a business motivation. He never felt it necessary to add his own name to the contract, a negligence which would be unthinkable today. His explanation for this oversight was that he wanted the Beatles to be free of any obligations to him, if they felt they would be better off elsewhere. His misgivings were understandable. He had no experience in artist management, nor any knowledge of the pop music business. In addition, his father and friends quickly pointed out that the childlike enthusiasm he'd shown for other ideas had been fleeting.

Brian abandoned his smart Ford Zodiac. He began careening around Merseyside in a hired van, much to the consternation of his parents, who failed to grasp why their respectable son was spending his evenings chauffeuring four rambunctious kids and their guitars between clubs and dance halls. His father was not concerned whether this group of boys might one day be bigger than Elvis. He felt Brian should be occupying himself with the family business. This type of adventurism into the shabby field of pop music, a province of upstarts and hustlers, was not very becoming. Most middle-class English parents would have agreed. Although it was 1962, nothing had occurred in Britain to delineate a new epoch. The country still languished in the conservatism of the 1950s, slowly shedding its last vestiges of empire. Not a single pirate radio station existed, and very few teen-agers were sneaking transistor radios into their bedrooms. Pop musicians were treated with the same sort of contempt that was reserved for actors in the Middle Ages. They were transients, no-goods, whose jingles were pleasing to the ear, though they couldn't be taken seriously.

If attitudes were being reshaped anywhere in Britain, it was in Merseyside. Epstein later admitted that he was in a unique position to observe these changes. As a record-store owner, he was certainly aware of the growing teen-age enthusiasm for beat music; he found he could predict fairly accurately the performance of a disc on the charts. He also took note of the devoted local followings that the various Liverpool groups, particularly the Beatles, had built up. If the Beatles were so popular locally, why shouldn't they be received as enthusiastically on a national scale? With this supposition in mind, he set to work to obtain a recording contract for them. However, the London record executives did not share his confidence and vision. They were steeped in searching for a profitable counterpart to America's Presley, or another crooning balladeer like Cliff Richard. Their main objection to the Beatles was that they thought no group had a chance of achieving stardom. Groups were simply passé. It was a narrative that Brian Epstein soon knew by heart, as he trekked despairingly around the record company offices.

His first move was to send a letter to Tony Barrow, a record reviewer for a Liverpool newspaper, whose literary talents were on loan at the time to the Decca Records publicity division. The letter asked Barrow to write about a local group, "which would one day be bigger than Elvis."

"I told him I couldn't write about them until they'd had a record released," says Barrow. "Then I said I'd be glad to, because I thought it would make good local news. Soon afterward, he brought me an acetate of the Beatles taken from a local TV documentary about the Cavern. It was cluttered with background noise and didn't sound too good, but I agreed to try and get him an audition for them on the strength of the acetate."

Barrow phoned the Decca marketing department, rather than the A&R (Artists and Repertoire) section, since Epstein was, after all, a respected record retailer, and he reasoned correctly that the marketing people would recognize the name of his record store. On this basis, the Beatles were granted an audition with Mike Smith, an A&R man.

"Smith liked the material and I was ready to write in my column that a local group had obtained a Decca contract," Barrow continued. "But Smith's superior, Dick Rowe, returned from the States, listened to the tapes and turned down the Beatles in favor of another group: the Tremeloes."

Epstein couldn't understand the decision. He sat patiently with the Decca executives and told them all about these boys. He explained that they were more popular with their local following than even established American pop stars. It was all to no avail. After several months of similar disappointments, he was ready to give up. He decided to make one final attack on the record companies. Armed with his bundle of acetates, he took the train to London again. This time, he managed to arrange an appointment with George Martin, an A&R man at Parlophone Records, at the time one of E.M.I.'s smaller labels. Martin had been working for the most part with comedy records; he had absolutely no experience with groups. But he liked the acetates and was impressed with Epstein's enthusiasm. The Beatles were invited for a recording test.

Although the session went well, the bureaucratic wheels of E.M.I. turned painfully slowly. The Beatles were back in Hamburg again when Brian finally received news that they'd been offered a contract. He went to London immediately and signed the agreement. It proved a great investment for E.M.I., but for the Beatles, just another unknown group, the financial reward was small. They were to receive one penny in royalties per single record sold. This meant that on an album of six tracks per side, they would make just six cents. For all their vast overseas sales, they would earn only half of this. E.M.I. also had an option to renew the contract for three successive years, during which time it had to increase the Beatles' royalties by the minuscule sum of one quarter of a penny at the end of the first year, and by one half a penny at the end of the second. The contract was typical of the deals that record companies were making at the time, grossly biased in their own favor. In fact, when the Beatles really began to sell huge quantities of records late in 1963, E.M.I., quite possibly noting its soaring profits, charitably raised their royalty per single to two cents.

"Love Me Do," their first single, was released in England in October 1962. It climbed slowly to the number seventeen position on the English hit parade, mainly on the strength of sales in the Liverpool area. When the Beatles became a household word a year later, the theory was bandied around entertainment business circles that Epstein had manipulated the progress of this first single by buying copies of the disc at stores where sales figures were taken to construct charts. Derek Taylor adamantly rejects this theory.

"Such behavior would have been contrary to Brian's very nature," he says. "That record, and all subsequent records, sold strictly on merit."

Although "Love Me Do" was only a moderate success, it provided Epstein with tangible proof of his group's potential, a reassurance which his seemingly unshakable confidence probably required. He decided it was time to unleash another of his discoveries onto the British public. Gerry and the Pacemakers' first single "How Do You Do It" became an immediate number one, as did the Beatles' second record "Please, Please Me."

A popular local brew was fast being transformed into a national brand. The chart success of these two groups had opened up an era of much wider recognition for any group hailing from Liverpool, but simultaneously it was a harbinger of doom for the city's beat scene. The best musicians were safely in the Epstein stable and inevitable envies reared their ugly heads among groups left behind. The fortunate Epstein bands were uneasy when they played in their home town. In new suits and ties, they were as embarrassed as if they were playing in their underwear. They felt guilty, as if they'd sold out.

Signs of ambition-induced conflict had appeared first among the Beatles. They went to Brian, like lieutenants to their captain, and demanded an execution. Their drummer, Pete Best, was to be the victim. Ringo Starr was brought in to replace him, and the Liverpool beat scene erupted in disgust at the dismissal.

Pete Best was not to share in the Beatles' wealth and success. Eventually, he went to work in a Liverpool bakery.

After his initial coups, Brian Epstein was now sought as a manager by many local musicians. He picked and chose as he pleased. Billy J. Kramer and the Dakotas, Cilla Black and the Fourmost were soon signed to Nems and went on to achieve varying degrees of success. Despite Epstein's sudden rise to such a commanding position in the British pop world, he insisted that each artist or group make it on merit.

"Brian would never play off the Beatles against other Nems artists," says Geoffrey Ellis. "No member of Nems' staff could say, 'If you book a less well-known artist, you might get the Beatles for the Christmas spectacular.' "

By the time "Please, Please Me" hit the charts, Nems' pilot was busily putting to use his promotional skills on a much larger scale. A series of press conferences and interviews were carefully arranged for his groups. Press handouts about the release of each recording were sent to the dailies as well as the music trade papers. The most novel feature of the announcements was that they subtly drew attention to selling points other than music—sense of humor, hair styles, clothes and personal charm. It was a technique unprecedented in British pop music, but in spite of it all, the Liverpool groups were ignored for a long time.

For the Beatles, the pace began to heat up early in 1963. They were playing the national theater circuit by this time and throughout the country they showed signs of becoming extraordinarily popular. They now had a full-time road manager, Mal Evans, formerly a bouncer at the Cavern. He had taken over the driving job from Neil Aspinall, a friend of the Beatles since their Hamburg days, who subsequently became their personal assistant.

"We were playing an incredible number of dates then," says Aspinall, a rugged, wiry individual with maniacal blue eyes. "Evans was scared stiff when he realized how fast he had to drive. I used to tell him, 'Mal, you don't have time to stay within the speed limits, just keep yer foot down.' He soon learned. Within a few months, he'd managed to collect three speeding fines.

"It's hard to say when Beatlemania really started. The boys became more popular after they'd had two number-one hits, but it was all a gradual buildup. I think it really started for us after we came back from a tour of Sweden in the autumn of '63. Then we noticed that the kids were really goin' wild, not just chalkin' on the van, but screamin' and hangin' onto yer."

Still the excitement was ignored by the British press. A few enterprising journalists wrote about the "Liverpool Sound," their own fabrication to account for a flood of successful Liverpool bands, but for the most part, the papers were busy relishing the exploits of Christine Keeler. For Tony Barrow, who had by now left Decca and was press officer at Nems, it was an uphill struggle. Only an occasional promotion handout made an inroad. The others found their way to the wastebaskets.

"There isn't much doubt that a fair amount of hype was used to promote the Beatles during this period," says Derek Taylor. "The exact number of pounds remains to be established. Epstein was very clever at putting over the Beatles and making it seem that they weren't interested in money. This showed even more when they went to America."

When the Beatles topped the British hit parade in August 1963, with "She Loves You," the song that brought "Yeah, yeah, yeah" to the forefront of the English vocabulary, the tradition-bound press still couldn't see the story. The papers remained blind to the social upheaval which the foursome were proliferating. Finally, in October, they were forced to take note when thousands of screaming fans besieged the London Palladium, where the Beatles' performance was being televised to a nationwide Sunday night audience. A few days later the London *Times* grudgingly relinquished a few inches of its precious column space to describe how forty Newcastle police took nearly an hour to restore order to a queue of thousands waiting to buy tickets for a Beatles' concert. At least some attention was being given to the pandemonium, if not the music.

Not until a few days before the end of 1963 did the *Times* consider Beatle music worthy of any serious discussion. The paper's music critic was very anxious to point out from the start that he was "not concerned with the social phenomenon of Beatlemania." He considered it a virtue that Lennon and McCartney wrote their own songs, which he described as "distinctly indigenous in character." With the usual fevered writing that one expects from the *Times,* he noted that Lennon and McCartney "think simultaneously of harmony and melody, so firmly are the major tonic sevenths and ninths built into their tunes . . . so natural is the Aeolian cadence at the end of 'Not a Second Time.' "

The lukewarm tribute came just in time. Within a few days the boys who resurrected the Aeolian cadence were to launch a cultural invasion upon the unsuspecting United States.

While British teen-agers were revelling in Beatle-induced euphoria, their American counterparts were slowly recuperating from the grievous loss of their short-lived idol, John Kennedy. The image of the glamorous "New Frontier," on which they were to have patterned their lives, had been obliterated, only to be replaced by a sour-faced, drawling Texan. As Lyndon Johnson intoned his political program, the gloom deepened. American youth, alienated by this patronizing style, became morbidly preoccupied with the future of its country. It would have clutched at any charismatic personality who offered a harmless diversion. In this case, the personality materialized in quadruplicate.

Brian Epstein had been planning to bring the Beatles to the United States for several months. He had made a deal on the phone with concert promoter, Sid Bernstein, for the group to make its debut at Carnegie Hall. Bernstein had called Brian in the fall of 1963, because he'd been reading the English papers and had taken a great interest in what was happening in England. In November, Brian flew to the States and persuaded Ed Sullivan to give the

Beatles top billing on his show, on the strength of their British chart success and the wide public recognition they were then beginning to achieve. Sullivan had recently visited in England and had seen the frantic scenes for himself, but he knew it was years since any British artist had had even a moderate success in the United States. He drove a hard bargain with Epstein, but Brian held out for top billing. The trivial sum of $2,400, which the Beatles were to receive for each appearance on the TV host's show, was less important to Epstein than the opportunity for the Beatles' visual image to appeal to huge numbers of people, not just teen-agers. It was the decisive maneuver in his plan to capture a market no less modest than the world.

However, there were certain other currents in the Beatles' favor which even Epstein couldn't predict. Aside from the escapist state of mind of American youth in the aftermath of the Kennedy assassination, two other unforeseeable circumstances contributed to the stupendous welcome which the United States extended to the Beatles. First of all, Capitol Records, E.M.I.'s American subsidiary, agreed to shell out $50,000 in advance publicity, a considerable sum of money for a music group unknown in the States. Capitol was also shrewd enough to concentrate its expense in New York, recognizing that if the investment paid dividends in the Big Town, the reverberations inevitably would be felt in the backwoods.

The second more complex contingency was that in 1964, seventeen-year-olds became the largest single age group in the United States for the first time in centuries. This phenomenon was the result of the sudden surge in the birth rate in the U.S. immediately after the Second World War. It meant that teen-agers, and specifically seventeen-year-olds, would become the center of population gravity for the seven years beginning in 1964.

Now that teen-agers were topping the demographic charts, they were bound to exert a much greater impact on the nation's tastes. Furthermore, almost half of them were still in school, outside adult society and without adult responsibility. They had lots of money to spend, most of it on leisure-time activities. By virtue of sheer numbers and spending power, American teen-agers now were more easily able to diffuse their causes, ideas and adolescent enthusiasms among other age groups. The timing of the Beatles' arrival in New York could not have been better.

The Capitol outpouring had started when "I Wanna Hold Your Hand" was released. The Beatle hype was hungrily devoured by the New York AM disc jockeys, who, with their usual bovine lack of discrimination, regurgitated it to the kids.

"Who's got the Beatles?"

"We've got the Beatles."

"W.A. Beatle. C." went the irritating jingles, growing ever more strident until February 7, 1964, when ten thousand teen-agers were so wound up that they cut school and stampeded out to Kennedy Airport with banners and buttons, to greet four very nervous Beatles. The TV cameras chased after the kids. Capitol's hype had succeeded beyond the company's wildest expectations, but the new teen-age masses were deciding what was going to be in the news. Whether the kids were brainwashed, or whether they made up their own minds, the youth decade was open for business.

One slightly older Beatle fan could scarcely wait for the group, or at least its manager, to arrive in the United States. Sid Bernstein had already trimmed several inches from his ample waistline by the time the Beatles' plane touched down to its tumultuous reception. His few thousand tickets had long been sold out and scalpers were having a field day, asking up to one hundred dollars for each precious piece of cardboard. Bernstein lost no time buttonholing Brian. He bundled him into a cab and took him over to Madison Square Garden, a hall which could accommodate over 20,000 people.

"I'd already called the Garden and found it was free the day after the Carnegie concert," says Bernstein. "The box office staff at Carnegie had told me that the demand for tickets was so great, we'd have no trouble filling Madison Square Garden with 20,000. I thought since we'd struck gold, we might as well clean up while it lasted. I really did a selling job on Brian trying to get him to okay the Garden. He stood in the empty hall, looked it over very carefully and said, 'Sid, let's leave this for next time.' There was no talking him out of it. He knew exactly what he was doing."

Although Sid Bernstein was rubbing his hands at his good fortune, the same could not be said of the management of the Plaza Hotel, one of the city's staider institutions. They had assumed that Messrs. Lennon, McCartney, Harrison and Starr were four respectable British businessmen. Their restraint was taxed to the limit as Beatle fans swarmed the fire escapes and hid in the bathrooms. Even some of their guests were struck down by bouts of Beatlemania. Rows of mounted police outside the Fifth Avenue exit, they were prepared to tolerate. Beatle wigs in the dining room, never.

Geoffrey Ellis remembers it all like a nightmare.

"The fans and police were battling outside, while the Beatles, imprisoned in their room, were watching TV with the sound turned off and at the same time listening to their recorded radio interviews. It was a very surrealistic scene."

The enthusiasm of the fans outside the Plaza was only equalled by the guests at a British Embassy party in Washington a few days later. The diplomatic set, too, was a little over-zealous with its welcome to the Liverpool boys. Beatlemania had evidently breached the class barriers.

"It was really an insult," says Neil Aspinall. "All these people were demanding autographs and then this drunken woman comes over to Ringo and tries to cut his hair." The incident was considered sufficiently scandalous that the British Foreign Secretary felt obliged to deny that any "manhandling" took place "The ambassador has in fact received a letter from a representative of the Beatles thanking him for a delightful evening," the Foreign Secretary's statement read. Brian Epstein was noted for his diplomacy.

The Beatles were even regarded as political ammunition by the British Prime Minister, Sir Alec Douglas-Home. A less likely Beatlemaniac is difficult to imagine. Addressing a Conservative Party rally, the chinless Sir Alec said: "A group of young men, using techniques which . . . I might not easily have acquired were making absolutely sure there would be no dollar crisis this year. . . . The Beatles are now my secret weapon. If any country is in deficit with us, I only have to say the Beatles are coming. . . ." It would scarcely have surprised the Conservatives if opposition leader, Harold Wilson, a politician renowned for his PR skills, had appeared in Parliament wearing a Beatle wig. After all, such an illustrious figure as John Paul Getty was wearing one.

Beatlemania fanned out over the American continent, encountering only token resistance. Victory was so absolute that any opposition at all was regarded as newsworthy. The gallant state education authorities of Connecticut made it clear that they could do without "borrowed hair styles" in their schools. One Connecticut student was suspended for wearing his hair in Beatle bangs and refusing to comb it to one side. The boy's father protested: "I don't believe my son is offending good taste. Besides, he isn't even a Beatle fan, he just likes to wear his hair in bangs."

While Beatlemania had risen in a steady tide in England, it submerged the United States in a deluge. Brian Epstein was overwhelmed by the gaggle of American wheeler-dealers, who wanted to share in the pillage. The descendants of the frontier medicine man clung to his coattails, pestered him with phone calls and pushed pens into his hand to try and secure his signature on a contract licensing them to produce some fatuous trinket bearing a vague similarity to one or all of the "fab four." Brian struggled to maintain his equilibrium as the bombardment increased. For a few days, the Beatles were secured for a handshake to say anything into a microphone. They rollicked about as if in an amusement park, lending their sponsorship to anything the DJs requested.

"America taught them one lesson," said Epstein. "Not to be taken for a ride. The DJs had a grand time but within a few days I had to stop it very severely."*

Epstein was also very careful to ration their personal appearances. Neil Aspinall says he weighed every offer for a Beatle performance. He refused to charge ten dollars a ticket for their Shea Stadium concerts, although

---

* *A Cellarful of Noise,* Souvenir Press.

American teen-agers' parents would have paid it, because he felt it was far too much and would be criticized as excessive. So tickets were from three to five dollars. Huge sums of money were turned down on many other occasions, whenever Brian felt that a particular booking would be detrimental to their career.

Burdened with so many other pressures ensuing from the Beatles' conquest of the United States, Epstein could well have done without the enormous legal and business tangle concerning the merchandising rights for Beatle goods. At first individual manufacturers had simply applied to Nems for marketing rights on an item which they wished to emblazon with Beatle pictures. About one hundred fifty such licenses already had been granted by Nems when, late in 1963, a group of people came up with the bright idea of acquiring as many of the overseas manufacturing rights on Beatle products as possible, in anticipation of worldwide Beatlemania.

Nems granted an English company, Stramsact, the right to issue licenses, permitting other companies to make articles bearing names, likenesses, photos and anything else pertaining to the Beatles. Stramsact had to pay Nems ten percent of all monies received within seven days of receiving payment. Early in 1964, another company, Seltaeb (Beatles spelled backwards), was incorporated in the United States and authorized by Stramsact to act as its agent. Certain persons were stockholders in both companies. The owners of Seltaeb shares were a group of six young Englishmen, bearing such aristocratic names as the Rt. Honorable Peregrine Eliot and Edward S. Miller-Mundy. The company's president was one Nicholas Byrne, described by a former Nems employee as "the biggest pain in the ass that Brian Epstein ever had to suffer."

Seltaeb's advance men received a tumultuous welcome in the United States from American businessmen. It may even have surpassed the greeting that the country's teen-agers gave the Beatles. For their part, the Seltaeb men knew how to drive a hard bargain; they held out for royalties of up to fifteen percent. The same formula was applied in other countries through which the Beatle whirlwind passed. Seltaeb advertised the rights in advance of the tour, sent a representative a few days before the Beatles' arrival, and as a formality, had a lawyer begin proceedings against any company already manufacturing Beatle products. Seltaeb's success was assured everywhere. The value of the world market for Beatle products was estimated at nearly $100 million. *The Wall Street Journal* predicted that Americans alone would spend $50 million on such goods. In retrospect, these figures were probably conservative estimates. One company, licensed by Seltaeb to produce Beatle clothing in the U.S., was claiming within two weeks of its contracts being signed that it had sold more than $2.5 million worth of such merchandise. The firm's president admitted it was the biggest promotion in its sixty-year history. Items sold included T-shirts, hats, beach shirts, tight pants and even tennis shirts, all embossed with pictures of the Beatles and their signatures. Another company was turning out 15,000 Beatle wigs a day and had a backlog of orders for over half a million. Several companies dispensed with the formality of acquiring a license to manufacture and lawsuits darkened the air. Seltaeb's fortunate president, Nicholas Byrne, was unperturbed. From behind his bottle of champagne in the Plaza Hotel, he stubbornly declined to predict how much money his firm was going to make, nor would he indicate how much of the monstrous takings would wind up in the Beatles' pockets.

Evidently, Brian Epstein did not approve of the amount of money that was accruing to Nems' licensees. In June 1964, a new agreement was signed with Stramsact, increasing Nems' share of the royalty from a mere ten to forty-five percent. Soon after, relations between Nems and its licensees deteriorated. Nems sued Seltaeb and Byrne for allegedly failing to return all of its agreed royalty to the company. The complaint also accused Byrne of using $100,000 of Seltaeb's gross income for personal expenses unrelated to the business affairs of Seltaeb. These included rents, chauffeured limousines, hotel bills and even loans of money to open charge accounts for female companions.

Byrne denied the allegations and asserted a counterclaim for over five million dollars, alleging that Nems, in breach of its agreement, had granted licenses to persons other than Seltaeb. The handling of merchandising rights had been delegated by Nems to a British theatrical lawyer, David Jacobs, a friend of Epstein's, who coincidentally committed suicide a few months after Brian died. Jacobs had handed over the responsibility to his assistant, says Nat Weiss, and there was a mix-up. The lawsuits whizzed back and forth.

Brian at first failed to appear in court in New York. His complaint was dismissed and Seltaeb obtained a default judgment for five million dollars. The default judgment eventually was set aside, but in the meantime another problem cropped up. The Beatles music publishing company, Northern Songs, was about to go public, and rather than have a lawsuit pending against Nems, Brian was advised to settle at a reasonable price. In the end, Nems' opponents took less than $100,000 in settlement for a libel suit and contract misunderstandings.

Geoffrey Ellis described the handling of the merchandising rights and the involvement with Seltaeb as a "glowing example of the unfortunate result of not being able to attend to everything at once."

"Some money was made on merchandising, but not as much as should have been made," he said. "Brian only had a small proportion of the merchandising rights. The professional advisers he'd used proved useless."

But Brian and the Beatles made plenty of money when the group began to play stadiums, especially in the United States. For their first Shea Stadium concert in New York, they earned $180,000. The concert was also a break in the clouds for its promoter, Sid Bernstein.

"Brian and I made the deal on the phone in January 1965," says Bernstein. "We agreed the Beatles would get $100,000 or sixty percent of the gate, whichever was higher. I didn't say anything about it for a long time, because Brian had asked me not to advertise before April 10. On that date I let the word out to a few reporters and the phones came off the wall. I didn't even have a formal contract, nor did I have $100,000, let alone even $10,000. I was in bad shape. I'd lost heavily on some other concert ventures. Carnegie Hall, a year ago, had just helped pay off some old debts. I asked Brian to draw up a contract, but by the time I heard from him again, I already had $180,000 in the bank on tickets sold. Brian had asked for $50,000 on signing and another $50,000 was payable about a month before the concert in August. When he sent me the contract, he was surprised to get the full $100,000 immediately. Of course, the final gate ran to 56,000 people. To hear twenty-eight minutes of screams, interspersed with some Beatle music, they paid over $300,000."

When the Beatles were bemoaning their financial situation a few years later, Bernstein offered them a million dollars for a single American concert. They turned him down. They were no longer interested in personal appearances; three years of touring had been exhausting enough. One of the Beatle entourage who endured all the tours was their personal assistant, Neil Aspinall. He admits he enjoyed it at the time, because he was young and had lots of energy, but he wouldn't want to go through it again.

"I've been all over the world, but I have a very strange impression of it," he says. "Japan, for me, was just a concert hall and a road to an airport. New York looked like the world's filing cabinet and even though I've been to Cincinnati, I couldn't tell you where it is. You stay in one town, one night. You have all the girls you want and everything else. Then, you're on to the next town and it's exactly the same.

"On the plane journeys, we'd spend most of the time playing cards. The games were often the best parts of the tour. Brian used to enjoy raising the stakes by about five times to scare his partners. Once, we were on a train going to Munich and he was losing about a hundred pounds to me. As we were getting near to Munich, he wanted to try and win some back quickly. He pulled out his cigarette lighter and said, 'Look, this is worth a hundred pounds. Let's make it double or quits.' I wanted to say no, but Don Short, a reporter with the *Daily Mirror*, kept egging Brian on to do it. So I agreed. Brian lost his lighter. Then he took off his gold watch. He said, 'This watch is a very good one. It's worth two hundred fifty pounds. Double or quits?' Again I didn't want to play the hand. I knew Brian stood a good chance of losing, but I didn't want him to think I wasn't giving him a chance to win his money back. He lost again. In the end I just settled for a hundred pounds.

"But, in general, Brian kept a cooler head than the rest of us. It was easier for him because he didn't have to stay in hotel rooms all the time. He'd be out working on the next tour, but the boys would be closeted in a hotel room, and they hated it, especially when they had days off between bookings and couldn't go anywhere. Then the rooms drove them crazy and there were lots of arguments.

"You felt like a criminal, always on the run. Our get-aways had to be very carefully planned. One night, I had a big argument with a stupid theater manager. I'd arranged for the limousine to be brought to the back of the theater as usual, but right near the end of the concert I found it was gone. The manager had decided that the boys would be leaving by the front entrance and he'd had the car moved. This was what they'd done for the president, he said. The people could then line the streets and wave at the car. I told the guy he was crazy. 'What about all those kids in the seats?' I said. 'They're not just going to sit there and wave, they'll kill us.' So I got the car 'round the back again and we escaped in our usual way. We'd let the audience expect an encore. The curtain would start to come down, but we wouldn't do an encore. We'd be off. We were in the car with the motor running, while the applause was still going on."

After three years it was understandable that the Beatles should have wanted to stop touring. They were expected to play only their hit songs, which in many cases had been recorded more than a year earlier. On a world tour the total number of songs in their repertoire would be no more than ten. Finally, they decided to stay home and make better records. It was then that "Sergeant Pepper" was recorded, when they'd had three months' rest after touring.

Nobody was more delighted when the tours ended than Wendy Moger, a veritable Mary Poppins to Brian and the Beatles for more than two years. She hated touring.

"The food was always bad. There was never any privacy and never anywhere to go to the loo," Wendy recalls. "The American tours weren't so bad because everything was pretty much taken care of, but Brian, Neil, Mal and I did the European tour on our own and we spent our lives running. We had to resort to all kinds of schemes to get the Beatles in and out of theaters and hotels. They thought it was very funny once that Brian and I were going in a police car. They didn't know that they were to be hidden in the back of a laundry van. We actually did get mobbed once in Chicago. It was a very frightening experience and it made me short-tempered with the crowds afterward. I got very angry with one girl just before a concert at the Cow Palace. I told her to get off the car. She leaned in the window and bit me. I still have the scar on my hand.

"The whole experience certainly opened my eyes. It gave me a great insight into the Beatles. Paul was always the spokesman, always the diplomat. John was very aloof. He'd take no nonsense from anyone and hated to have to do anything for publicity reasons. George was still very shy at this time, though I know he's more confident now. Ringo was very sweet. He was always the most gallant. With all that pressure, he still treated me like a lady."

The tours weren't *Satyricon* on the road, as far as Derek Taylor is concerned. He disagrees with Lennon, who described them as such.

"They, and myself too, were provincial Englishmen, continually being surprised and shocked by the big bad world, or what little they saw of it," he says. "I thought the road tours were very dull."

Taylor did not accompany them on their last two tours in 1966, both of which were far from dull. The first outing took them to the Philippines. After a concert in Manila, the Beatles were invited to visit the presidential palace. Tony Barrow remembers that Brian didn't give a direct answer that evening. He said he would reply to the invitation the next day.

"While we were watching TV that night, we saw a news item that surprised us," says Barrow. "The palace dignitaries were waiting for the Beatles to show up. The next edition of Manila's newspapers carried the headline: BEATLES SNUB PRESIDENT.

"There was a general uproar and Brian was invited to go on TV the next evening and explain what had happened. But, for some reason, his speech was drowned by terrible interference, and nobody could make out what he said. Sentiment was running so strongly against the Beatles that we actually had the feeling their lives might be in danger."

The Beatles took a lot of abuse at the airport. They were booed, jeered and insulted by airport officials, as well as the public, while they filled out their departure forms. But the Philippines incident was only a ripple compared with what was to occur on their last American tour.

John Lennon had been interviewed in England by Maureen Cleave of the London *Evening Standard*. One of his remarks had concerned the popularity of Jesus Christ compared to the Beatles. Reports of the statement eventually reached the United States, where naturally they had a much greater impact. The comment began to make headlines about a week before the Beatles were due to start an American tour. One state senator, Robert Fleming of Pennsylvania, declared he was going to try to have the Beatles banned. His statement helped to fan the bonfires of Beatle records, still smoldering in the Bible Belt when the group arrived in the country. However, it was decided that the tour would go on. The Beatles' first engagement was in Chicago and Lennon was to give a press conference before the concert to explain his remarks. It was held in Tony Barrow's hotel room.

"The room was so jammed with reporters and TV cameras, you could only just squeeze in through the door," says Barrow. "John had to face an incredible battery of equipment. When he walked into my room, it was the only time I ever saw him look frightened."

The first concert in the South took place in Memphis on a tense August evening. Some debris was hurled at the Beatles during the concert and six Ku Klux Klansmen picketed outside the Mid-South Coliseum. For Tony Barrow, standing in the wings, the worst moment was when a firecracker exploded in the audience.

"Each Beatle just glanced at the others to see if one of

them would drop," Barrow recalls. "It says something for them that they didn't miss a note."

The 1966 American tour proved altogether too strenuous. Nat Weiss says it wasn't surprising it was the last one.

"Brian told me it was the end in San Francisco, just before they played," he says. "He was dejected. 'This will be the last Beatle concert ever,' he said. He knew it was inevitable and he was all for stopping it. We'd just been through a very bad experience in Cincinnati. The promoter had been trying to save himself a few cents by not putting a roof over the stage. It started to rain and the Beatles couldn't go on because they would have been in danger of electrocution. They had to turn away 35,000 screaming kids, who were all given passes for a concert the next day. The strain had obviously been too much for Paul. When I got back to the hotel, Paul was already there. He was throwing up with all this tension.

"We were stuck in Cincinnati for a day. I was sharing a suite with Brian and our bedrooms were at opposite ends of a huge central area. In the morning, I was awakened by all this noise. I walked out of the bedroom to find about a hundred people sitting around in our suite. They'd been told that if they wanted to see the Beatles, they should wait in Mr. Epstein's suite. I called the police and had them all chased out, but I was terrified until the police arrived. Brian was known to sleep in the nude and I had visions of him marching in on this crowd. We were very glad to leave Cincinnati.

"There were usually sixty or seventy people on these tours and it was always amusing to see who would pair off with whom. Brian and I used to sit in the back of the plane and try to guess who would form couples. There've never been tours like the Beatles' tours before or since. I've been on tours since, when we've been held up by crowds of kids, and I've tried to explain to people who think it's a difficult situation, that this is nothing."

The end of the tours was the end of an era for the Beatles. On the plane back to London after the last concert, George told Tony Barrow: "Well, I guess that's it. I'm not a Beatle anymore."

Neil Aspinall is convinced that the end of touring was really the beginning of the breakup. While they were touring they were a close-knit unit. Despite personality differences and arguments, they held tight. Now for the first time, they had a chance to settle down and develop their own individual interests.

"The boys went through a lot of shit together on those tours, just like guys would go through if they went to war together," says Aspinall. "It was like guys returning from Vietnam. When they get back, one lives in Brooklyn and the other lives in the Bronx, but they rarely socialize. Why? Because they were very different people to begin with, but they were obliged to stay together for a long time."

Even before 1966, the personality differences had become evident. Friends say John and Paul were often diametrically opposed in their attitude toward social acceptability. John rejected it all. He was embarrassed about the Beatles' collar-and-tie image. Paul, however, clung to anything upper-middle class. Their views differed, for example, over the M.B.E. awards. John would be irritated whenever anybody mentioned it, but Paul regarded it as a great honor.

The award of the M.B.E.s to the Beatles caused quite a ruckus in England. Most of the protests against the bestowal of the medals on pop musicians came from people who'd distinguished themselves militarily in either the First or the Second World War. It seems they were not impressed with the Beatles' conquests. Several of the protesters returned their medals to the Queen. Among them was a certain Colonel Frederick Wagg. He received some fan mail, according to the following article which appeared in the London *Times*:

Colonel Frederick Wagg, the 73-year-old retired Royal Artillery officer who returned his war medals to the Queen in protest against the award of the M.B.E. to the Beatles, has received letters from all parts of the world—including one "stamped" with trading stamps.

Many have been sent to him care of Buckingham

Palace, and a member of the Royal Household has been forwarding them to the Colonel at Old Park House, Old Park Avenue, Dover. One letter brought the Colonel into conflict with the Post Office.

The letter was from an anonymous group of Beatle fans. It was postmarked Forest Hill, London, but the only stamps on it were half-a-dozen trading stamps. The envelope was marked: "Waggy will pay the postage."

John and Paul, however, were diverging on issues other than the M.B.E. awards. One person very well acquainted with them both at the time was John Donbar, Marianne Faithfull's first husband. Donbar was a Cambridge student who'd spent his summers in the early sixties drifting around the United States, where he'd come into contact with such luminaries as William Burroughs, Bob Dylan and Gregory Corso. In other words, he was sufficiently "hip" to impress the Beatles. Donbar's parents were close friends with another upper-middle-class family from London's West End: the Ashers.

"Paul met Jane Asher before the Beatles had a number-one hit," says Donbar. "She was emceeing a pop show on British TV in which they appeared. Jane Asher's mother is a music professor at the Royal College of Music in London. She'd encouraged her children to take an active interest in show business. Very soon, Paul moved into the Ashers' house on Wimpole Street.

"Mrs. Asher had a lot of influence on Paul. In many ways she was a substitute mother to him, because his own mother was dead. She regarded him as very spoiled, but treated him very well. Jane is a pretty girl with very definite upper-middle-class values. My impression of the situation was that Paul was going out with the landlady's daughter. Being from a good family, Jane satisfied his need for security, stability and respectability.

"For several years, Paul was also very close to my kid's nanny. He saw her on and off for ages. She was a very earthy, working-class girl, unlike Jane. Since he married Linda Eastman, I haven't seen him at all. I believe he may have found the sort of security he was looking for.

"I really got to know John much later, probably not until 1965. My pad was the center for a lot of scenes in those days and I took hundreds of acid trips with John. It was John who put up much of the money for that full-page 'legalize marijuana' appeal in the *Times*. I was helping to organize that.

"The break between John and Paul is fairly easy to explain. Paul was getting more and more into this upper-middle-class syndrome, and all that went with it, and John was getting further and further out. After 1965, he became a lot crazier. He really loosened up and he didn't give a shit about anything. He was incredibly generous and he'd pay for any idea that appealed to him. Paul was always cautious about doing anything new, especially when it came to drugs. He was just scared of stepping away from the value system he was aspiring to. They both spent a lot of time at my pad. John once described me as the leader of a London underground clique, which I'd say was hardly true. It was just that a lot of ideas seemed to get going at my place.

"George, I still see occasionally. He's become much more confident. He was always a bit shy and felt a little inferior because he was the youngest. Both John and Paul tended to dominate him. I think the reason I got on with them was that I didn't treat them as Beatles, because at this time they wanted to stop being Beatles and be themselves."

They may have wished to stop being Beatles, but the world wasn't prepared for this eventuality. Three years of monstrous success and seeming infallibility couldn't be erased overnight. Youth wanted the myth to continue.

CHAPTER FOUR

Consciousness Expansion and
the Death of Brian Epstein

The Beatles gave their last live concert in San Francisco on August 29th, 1966. It brought to an end nearly four years of touring since the release of their first record. The decision to quit was to have major repercussions on all of their lives. The Beatles had been extricated from any normal maturing process and exposed to many incredible strains. They had been obliged to maintain a public image of "nice boys," which was becoming a struggle, especially for John. Even so, Epstein's protectiveness had cushioned them effectively from all harsh realities.

They felt nothing but contempt for the screaming, frenzied audiences they'd faced for so long. The time had come to be recording artists, rather than performers. They wanted to rest and develop their own individual interests. The money they'd made from personal appearances had been considerably greater than earnings they'd obtained from record sales, because of the small royalty rate received under the terms of their first record contract. Now they were about to negotiate a new contract with E.M.I., giving them a better deal. Under the first contract, they had earned only a few pennies per album. The new agreement, signed in January 1967, secured for them 10 percent of the album's wholesale price, and 17½ percent in the most important market, the United States.

The record industry generally had recently begun to reward its artists with better terms. Record companies' sales had undergone a rapid increase in the last few years, as American youth paid greater attention to pop music. With the emergence of the San Francisco sound, and the realization by a few entrepreneurs that fortunes could be made virtually overnight in the record industry, the bidding for rock groups became cutthroat. Even an unknown artist was being offered as much as $50,000 on signing and a seven or eight percent royalty based on the wholesale price of his record, terms which were much more advantageous than those offered to the Beatles back in the dark ages of 1962. It was no wonder that, having contributed a very healthy chunk to E.M.I.'s profits for several years in return for comparatively little, the Beatles were now demanding a royalty rate commensurate with their status and selling-power in the record industry.

But by no means were they short of cash because of the previously low record royalty. Music publishing is a lucrative field, and the Beatles, especially John and Paul, owned a large stake in Northern Songs, the company which published their compositions. Except for a few songs on their very first albums, the Beatles only recorded their own compositions. With Northern Songs receiving from E.M.I. about twenty-five cents in mechanical royalties per Beatle album sold, the publishing company's profits soared. In addition, Northern grew richer by about five cents every time a Beatles' song was played on the radio. Touring hadn't been the group's only source of substantial income. Music publishing had added vast sums to the Beatle coffers, compensating for the pittance they'd obtained from E.M.I. in record royalties up to 1967.

Although the new royalty rate allowed them to earn as much money without touring, there were other, non-monetary reasons for retiring from the road. Some of their music on "Revolver," recorded just before their final tour, had become too difficult to perform live. Now they would be free from the obligation to reproduce their songs through the rickety public address systems of the world's sports arenas. They could make records as complex as they wished. Their art would be free to develop a new direction.

During the previous four years, the Beatles had revolutionized pop music. In the 1950s, most pop songs were written in music publishers' offices in New York (hit factories) by a task force of writers, who were generally treated like assembly-line workers. With the most basic musical instruments, often only a piano and a wooden box for a drum, they would churn out a number of demonstration discs, one of which might be selected by the record company for its latest, oily, teen-age idol, because it had an attractive opening phrase about a goddess in high heels. The Beatles de-industrialized this aspect of pop music. They established beyond question the premise that writing and performing popular songs was an art form. Rock became credible with intellectuals, because even the most highbrow music critic had to admit that the Beatles' songs were good. Hit records could no longer be denigrated simply because they were commercially successful products. The high quality of Beatle records was evident, even if they did appeal to a huge public market. Nor did the Beatles want to stand still and reap a quick financial reward by exploiting a currently popular formula. They were musical innovators, anxious for their art to progress.

By 1966, the Beatles dwelt in the same rarified atmosphere as presidents and royalty. They had so advanced popular music that for a large contingent of youth, especially in the United States, rock was no longer just a fashionable interest, but was viewed as the cornerstone for a new way of life. American youth was at last shedding its Bermuda shorts and forgetting to go to the barber's. FM radio stations began to proliferate throughout the country and rock music was soon being administered in massive doses to the youth. Sales figures for records give a reliable indication of the impact of this assault via the air waves. Within two years, they rose by $200 million to over one billion dollars. Only one other ingredient was necessary before American youth proudly proclaimed it had initiated an alternate culture. The Beatles were to help popularize that ingredient as well.

In the late fifties, the Liverpool group had frequently taken amphetamines in order to survive the long, exhausting hours of playing in Hamburg's clubs. They had no contact with marijuana until they came to the States in 1964. Grass was virtually unheard of in England at this time. From grass, the Beatles soon graduated to other drugs. In the summer of 1966, John and George had their first experience with LSD. They had known of Brian Epstein's involvement with the drug for some time and had been curious to learn about his experiences with it. Their own initiation occurred in London when a dentist friend of George's slipped them some one night at a dinner. Some time went by before they had their second trip, but early in 1967 their acid experiences became more frequent, especially after touring stopped. Paul McCartney was the last Beatle to take it. His cautious reluctance was finally broken down as the group began recording its acid-inspired masterpiece, "Sergeant Pepper," early in 1967.

"We were into acid nearly a year before it reached most of the kids," says Neil Aspinall. "Everybody thought we were just starting to take acid in 1967 when 'Pepper' was made. But 'Pepper' was really the culmination of our acid days. By the time 'Sergeant Pepper' was released and all the kids in Haight-Ashbury started taking acid, we were into something else."

Among the Beatles and their entourage, a certain social prominence is attached to being the first to take LSD, as if the distinction of being an early initiate implies that you were an artistic or cultural leader of the time. Lennon rarely misses an opportunity to put down McCartney and even Aspinall because they were slower than he to capitulate to the hallucinogenic powers of the drug. One thing is certain. After his initial experiences with LSD, Paul McCartney became convinced that "Sergeant Pepper," with its many drug connotations, was a work of great artistic and social significance. Nat Weiss says it was Paul who insisted that the album should have an expensive and complicated cover, featuring all the people the Beatles admired.

McCartney also began to take a much greater interest in the group's business affairs at the time. George Harrison claims that Paul wasn't happy with the new royalty rate which had been obtained from E.M.I. He complained that another group, then being managed by one Allen Klein, presumably the Rolling Stones, was earning more money than the Beatles, even though they sold fewer records.

Whether McCartney was dissatisfied with Brian Epstein or not, Brian certainly went to great lengths to please him. Epstein's friends say Paul frequently pestered Brian with trivial details and Brian was always anxious to be accommodating. In his autobiography, Epstein said of McCartney: "Paul can be temperamental and moody and difficult to deal with but I know him very well and he me. This means that we compromise on our clash of personalities. He is a great one for not wishing to hear about things and if he doesn't want to know, he switches himself off, settles down in a chair, puts one booted foot across his knee and pretends to read a newspaper, having consciously made his face an impassive mask."*

It was quite a task to obtain legal clearance from all the celebrities whom the Beatles planned to portray on the "Sergeant Pepper" cover. Brian managed to persuade Wendy Moger to take on the job, although she had not been his personal assistant for some months.

"He asked me to try and get legal clearance from everybody within a week," said Wendy. "E.M.I. wasn't very keen on the cover, but Paul wanted to do it. It was an incredible job. I spent many hours and pounds on the telephone to the States. Some people agreed to it, others wouldn't. Fred Astaire was very sweet about it, but Shirley

---

* *A Cellarful of Noise,* Souvenir Press.

Temple wanted to hear the record first. I got on famously with Marlon Brando."

While the cover for "Sergeant Pepper" was causing so many people headaches, McCartney had also dreamed up the idea of Apple, which was soon to develop into a headache of his own.

"I remember when he first mentioned it to me," says Nat Weiss. "Brian didn't have any time for the idea because he was very busy trying to consolidate Nems. He had just gone out of his way early in April to ensure that Paul's first private visit to the United States went well."

April 1967 was a busy month for Paul McCartney. He made his grand announcement that he took LSD and then followed up his statement with various comments suggesting that he couldn't be responsible if other people blindly followed his example. A number of people lost no time in lashing him for his boldness. An outraged Billy Graham warned America that the statement might encourage young people to believe that they could have a "great religious experience" through LSD, because McCartney had said he came nearer to God after taking the drug. Graham advocated that LSD should be "shunned like the plague" by young people. He did not specify if this was because they might not be able to handle the effects of a bad trip, or if his objections were based on a clash of religious views.

The following month Brian Epstein was quoted in *Queen* Magazine as saying: "There is a new mood in the country and it has originated through hallucinatory drugs. I am wholeheartedly on its side." Epstein's statement was even discussed in the British Parliament. It may be an indication of his credibility with the powers-that-be that neither he, nor any of the Beatles, was ever "busted" during his lifetime. The powers perhaps were confident of his abilities to keep a rein on the Beatles.

"At this time, Brian didn't see the Beatles as often as he used to," says Nat Weiss. "They socialized much less. Brian used to say that they were into the acid scene too much, though he was taking it too, which was something I could never understand. In May, I went to England and Brian gave a huge party at his house in Sussex. John

Lennon arrived in his psychedelic Rolls Royce, bringing with him lots of LSD. That night many well-known show business personalities were turned on for the first time."

That same month, the Beatles' drug-inspired "Sergeant Pepper" crashed onto the scene in a new wave of imagery and color. The album, which had taken four months to complete, was the grand overture to the summer of flowers and love. "A splendid time was guaranteed for all," the Beatles announced. Their consummate interest in drugs and psychedelic fashion was being offered to the world. It was a summer such as London had never experienced before. The "Swinging London" portrayed in Antonioni's film *Blow-Up* was already a widely accepted myth. In the imaginations of the many foreign visitors who descended upon the British capital that year, London had acquired the glamor once associated with Hollywood. The sudden arrival of so many tourists, more than any other single factor, expedited this myth and allowed it to prosper. Since Beatlemania had swept the United States, all things English had become the vogue. As early as 1965, the "fab" fashion centers of Carnaby Street and King's Road had become tourist attractions. Together with the arrival of the mini-skirt, they inaugurated a clothes consciousness that raised London to the forefront of the fashion world. So it was no surprise when the Beatles, as trend-setters, decided to invest in the fashion boom.

The summer of 1967, a summer of rare good weather, was the start of London's awakening. Beads, bells and flowers proliferated, as did LSD. There was a burst of activity on the live music scene. Two new rock theaters opened, the Roundhouse and the Middle Earth, and Brian Epstein staged some of his best rock shows at the Saville Theater. Indian musical instruments and outlandish clothes joined forces to produce the Incredible String Band. John Peel's dulcifying tones occupied the air waves. Stroboscopes were the rage. The Beatles' flights of fantasy had carried over to a large section of London's youth, but at least their indulgences stayed within the bounds of sanity.

The release of "Sergeant Pepper" provoked a less lyrical reaction in the United States, especially among the freewheeling California youth. By 1966, dozens of local bands had established themselves in San Francisco, spawning a new music scene. The Family Dog were throwing dances at the Avalon Ballroom and an enterprising friend of many groups was staging benefit concerts for the San Francisco Mime Troupe. Bill Graham, German-Jewish refugee with a picturesque vocabulary, soon left the Mime Troupe and began to produce rock concerts on a full-time basis. He opened a concert hall in San Francisco's black ghetto, the dilapidated Fillmore district. For a while, the city's music scene flourished. The Bay Area's new generation of flower children waved peace signs at each other and lolled around in the sunshine in Golden Gate Park. Their carefree way of life was reflected in the music of the Jefferson Airplane, the Grateful Dead and the girl with the big voice, Janis Joplin.

In one sector of the city, Haight-Ashbury, a community of bohemians, opting for an escape from the competitive aggressions of the American way of life, had resurfaced and been rechristened "hippies." Unfortunately, their new environment did not remain uncontaminated for long.

In June 1967, more than 30,000 people turned up for the Monterey Pop Festival. There were no large-scale "freak outs" or bad trips at Monterey. The police turned a blind eye to the marijuana that was being smoked. But after the concert the word about California was out. That summer, thousands of teen-agers dropped out of high schools and colleges throughout the country and headed out to San Francisco to become hippies. Within a few months, LSD and speed were being consumed on an unparalleled scale.

Thousands of pimply-faced high-school kids soon deduced that "Sergeant Pepper" was LSD inspired. Those that didn't were enlightened by *Time* Magazine. The cult heroes were popularizing acid and psychedelia, and inevitably, the initiates were going to follow. There was no better place to get stoned than in San Francisco, where the "vibes" were so good. Kids who had never smoked a marijuana cigarette in their lives were dropping acid and taking speed. The Haight-Ashbury people struggled to cope with the inundation, but the invasion was overwhelming. The free medical clinics and free food stores were unable to handle the volume. By the time many teenagers returned to their suburban hometowns at the end of their vacations, Haight-Ashbury was in ruins. Drug use had caught up with the drug orientation of rock and the fusion of the two was beginning to take place in the consciousness of a generation. "Pepper" had finally bridged the gap, right down to suburbia.

The Beatles' influence on the tastes and habits of American youth had started when the "fab" foursome first appeared on thirty million American TV screens in 1964. Then, the nation's psychologists scurried to uncover an explanation to account for the hysteria of its youth. As the Beatles' songs became more sophisticated, a generation began to extract a new set of values from their music. The Beatles emphasized the "now," concentrating on the senses, and American youth plunged into the experiences which Beatle music proffered as a new and more attractive alternative to the scrubbed-neck values of American parents.

Were the Beatles trend-setters, or did they merely help to popularize certain things by lending them the magnitude of their names? When John Lennon sang: "Help me if you can I'm feeling down," his lyrics were interpreted as a sensitive reflection of the pervasive mood of the day. But when the Beatles sang: "Picture yourself in a boat on a river with tangerine trees and marmalade skies," an entire generation was propelled into flights of fantasy. John says he was thinking of Alice in Wonderland when he wrote that line.

John Donbar, their former friend, is convinced that they weren't trend-setters.

"The Beatles, all of them, are very naïve in many ways," he says rather disparagingly. "I saw them influenced by all sorts of nonsense a number of times. In general, they went along with everything that was happening in the sixties. They made fine music, sure. But their names were linked to acid, and it was assumed that they were leaders in this field too."

Even if they weren't trend-setters, for much of the youth in the sixties, the Beatles were the "four wise men."

They were the heralds of an alternate culture, a belief which anguished American parents, repulsed by all this drug taking and wild music, only helped to propagate. Youth's involvement with rock and dope brought about a polarization of the two generations, which was to culminate in the United States with the 1969 Woodstock Festival. For the first time on good old American TV, millions of equally good old American parents were forced to witness the spectacle of their children swallowing huge quantities of drugs, shaking their chubby bottoms to loud music and lying around in the mud, from which American parents had been trying to keep them all their lives with large, healthy doses of soap. With rock and dope, sixties youth felt it had new ammunition with which to go beyond the more traditional forms of social rebellion such as the *Look Back in Anger* variety of the fifties. They saw a new honesty reflected in the new music. This was justified to a certain extent, at least in urban centers such as London, New York and San Francisco, where legitimate new attitudes were finding outlets for their expression in music.

Until 1967, the Beatles sang about simple, honest emotions and the kids absorbed it all and identified with it. But "Sergeant Pepper" was the product of a more abstract consciousness, which, rather than simply portraying life in music, abstracted lifelike situations and put them into more metaphysical terms. It was an attempt at a pure, freestanding work of art, and the Beatles, as artists, wanted it to be accepted as that. But the kids tried to identify with their heroes' music, just as they had done in the past, with the result that life began to imitate art. "Sergeant Pepper" broke with the conventional, yet unwittingly established a convention of its own. Without knowing why, the great vacuous mass of American teen-agers decided it was supposed to have all these new things, with which the Beatles seemed to be involved. They wanted costumes, Salvation Army band coats, bells, beads, painted faces and all the other absurd paraphernalia. The average youngster in Des Moines saw a picture of John Lennon wearing flowered pants and immediately ran out and bought himself a pair. He was not concerned that they were mass-produced by the Handy Dandy Manufacturing

Corporation of Seventh Avenue, nor did he wonder why they just happened to be in stock in Aunt Francis' Dry Goods Store. Aunt Francis didn't know they were a "hot item." She'd only been told they'd sell by a guy in New York.

The institutions had grabbed hold of these signs of a new way of living and translated them into their own terms. It had taken a while for the new trends to filter down to those who control the elements of mass change. Now they understood. To have expected them to assimilate their policies with any new consciousness would have been like expecting a square peg to slot into a round hole. They just adjusted their machinery slightly and out came a new batch of products, catering to the "hippie." The Peter Max era was under way. Everything "groovy" could be mass-produced. It didn't even need to be advertized. The media took care of that. With its single-minded concern for the mass market, television, radio and magazines reduced the values of a new culture to a level which the typical American consumer could understand.

Left to their own devices, the Beatles had really triggered something. They could never have guessed its consequences.

Brian Epstein didn't go to the Beatles' last concert in San Francisco. He stayed at his hotel in Beverly Hills and there he underwent an experience which disturbed him considerably. Nat Weiss was staying with him at the hotel.

"Brian and I had gone out to dinner, but when we returned to the hotel our briefcases had been taken," said Weiss. "We received a ransom note threatening to expose Brian because of certain letters and pills that were in the case. I called the police and the guy was arrested. It turned out to be the same boyfriend of Brian's who had held him up at knifepoint and taken his briefcase before. Once again, Brian wouldn't press charges. It wasn't that he really cared about the stigma this time, but he just felt very sorry for the boy.

"The next month Brian tried to kill himself. Everybody said he was depressed because it was the end of touring, but I knew a lot of his depression was due to what had

73

happened in Beverly Hills. If there was something else ailing him, I can only assume that it was a more complex personal frustration. He took an overdose of pills after leaving notes saying that his friends, Peter Brown, Geoffrey Ellis and I, should have his property. Fortunately, they brought him to a hospital in time. He did try and make another attempt a few months later, but it was a very halfhearted one. I think he was losing confidence in himself. Some of his predictions, usually so infallible, were not working out. He was also heavily into LSD at this time. He became very difficult to work with, when he came back to the States in October."

Although a vast amount of work was already consuming his energy, Epstein wanted to involve himself in even more ambitious projects. Weiss says he was still keen to prove that he was a good manager, and that managing the Beatles so successfully hadn't just been a fluke. He was also looking for something to satisfy his artistic bent. For a long while, he considered putting on plays at the Saville Theater, though eventually he decided to use the premises for rock concerts.

"He wasn't at all worried that the theater had to be run at a loss," says Weiss. "He knew he was making plenty of money from management fees from the Beatles and other artists. He left the running of Nems to his staff for the most part. Brian simply liked the idea of presenting the very best American artists in England. He brought over Chuck Berry, Fats Domino and the Four Tops. Of course, he had to pay them all American wages. But Brian loved to surround himself with the very best musicians. He had his own bar at the Saville. It became a gathering place for English and American rock celebrities."

Brian continued to take new groups under his management. He had plans to place his many artists under a much wider managerial umbrella, a scheme that it seems he was devising in order to allow himself more time to concentrate on the Beatles and his own artistic aspirations. Weiss says part of the problem with many of his new groups was that they weren't satisfied to be anything less than superstars in the shortest possible time.

Epstein's plan to expand his management organization

involved Nat Weiss, Robert Stigwood, his new co-managing director and Sid Bernstein, who by now was himself managing artists. Brian arranged for all four to meet at New York's Waldorf Astoria Hotel in April 1967.

"It was the last time I saw him," says Bernstein. "He wanted me to become his partner in the States with Nat Weiss. Stigwood and he would run the London end of the business. I was to bring in the Rascals and the Blues Project, which I was then managing. Brian would throw all his artists into the pot—except the Beatles. I turned down the deal, although he wanted to do it very badly. I didn't see what I really stood to gain, if the Beatles were excluded. The Bee Gees and Cream, both with Nems, hadn't yet started to happen. Cilla Black hadn't got off the ground either. Brian gave me a ride downtown in his limousine after the meeting. I felt very concerned about him because he looked just awful. There was no doubt that he was terribly unhappy. I asked him what was wrong. He said, 'I just don't feel well, I feel sick.' "

That same day Epstein took a heavy dose of Seconals, prior to his Murray the K. interview. Even with the drugs, he made some remarkably accurate predictions about who would be the next big star in rock.

"When you have Jimi Hendrix [in the United States], I'm sure you'll like him," Epstein declared. "Jimi has just broken through in England. He'd been around the Village for a long time, but nobody took any interest in him. He's much better than 'Hey, Joe.' It's not a gimmick that he can play a guitar with his teeth, it's just that he's an ace guitarist."

Epstein also had a few words to say about that poor, plastic reproduction of the Beatles, the Monkees.

"I, as a manager, can't help but admire what was done with the Monkees, even though I couldn't have done it myself, because I'm not that sort of person."

And on the Beatles themselves: "I don't think you'll ever get me to say that they will never appear in public again, but how can they progress in a series of tours? There's no reason why they will never appear in public again, but I don't think they will appear in the context of the previous terms.

"Some people are terribly good at personal appearances. The Beatles? I don't think they were really that great on stage. They just projected their personalities well.

"At the moment, they are doing great things in the studio ["Sergeant Pepper" was being recorded]. They take longer now, of their own volition, to make records. They're hyper-critical of their own work. Paul rang me up just the other day and said he wanted to make one small change to a track."

Only a few months previously, Brian had been despairing of what to do for the Beatles, now that they'd stopped touring. But by this time, he seemed to have very definite ideas. He told the DJ that they were going to make a film, though the idea needed developing and they still had to find a director. The film was *Magical Mystery Tour,* the Beatles' first-experienced failure. It was not made until after Epstein's death. Overestimating their talents as filmmakers, the Beatles decided not to employ an independent director, a contingency that Brian Epstein's artistic guidance almost certainly would have precluded. The resulting film was an amateurish home movie.

Although Epstein still exercised his guidance over the Beatles' careers, before he died he had at least begun to allow them more contact with the world-at-large, from which he had kept them shielded for so long. In July they went off to Greece to buy an island, an idea Brian disapproved of, but with which he went along. Giving the Beatles a free rein was a hard decision for Brian, who was still devoted to them and wanted to protect them at all costs. For years, they had been the center of his attentions. He even carried photographs of them in his briefcase, along with the telegrams he sent them when they were awarded a record contract.

"His favorite picture of John was one of him lying on his back drinking from a bottle of wine," says Nat Weiss. "There's been a lot of nonsense spoken that the Beatles intended to leave Brian when their contract with him expired, but he never doubted that they'd stay with him. McCartney had been difficult at times, yet they became very friendly shortly before Brian's death."

Epstein did have something to take his mind away from

the Beatles' moves toward more independence. In July his father died and Brian spent several weeks with his bereaved mother. Her unhappiness allowed him to feel he was needed by somebody, as he made clear in a letter to Nat Weiss:

My Dear Nat:

Thanks so much for the cable. It was nice of you and very comforting.

I'm coming to New York, September 2nd. I'd have come earlier, but my Father's passing has given me the added responsibility of Mother.

The week of *Shiva* is up tonight and I feel a bit strange. Probably been good for me in a way. Time to think and note that at least now I'm really needed by Mother. Also time to note that the unworldly Jewish circle of my parents' and brother's friends are not so bad. Provincial maybe, but warm, sincere and basic. I'm going back to London tomorrow Monday and returning Friday. After all, although my Father was sixty-three (a little young to die I think) she's only fifty-two and must find a new life. They were very devoted. She knew nothing else. (married him at eighteen) and had nearly thirty-four years happy marriage. (must be good) So you see I must do all I can. . . .

Brian was also very enthusiastic about a trip that he was going to make to Canada. He was to emcee a Canadian TV series of variety shows, an opportunity that he felt would allow him to be recognized as a personality in his own right, instead of simply being known as a manager and concert promoter. He was again working very hard. Neil Aspinall says he was worried that Brian might be overtiring himself, because he'd been in hospital in recent months.

"I went over to see him one night, a few days before he died," says Aspinall. "I was going to tell him he should be taking it easy and that there was no reason he should be working this hard, but he was too busy to see me."

On August 25, the Beatles went to Bangor to be indoctrinated in transcendental meditation. Brian had decided to spend the weekend at his country house in Sussex with Geoffrey Ellis and Peter Brown. Some of Brown's friends were supposed to arrive Friday night, but they didn't show up until late. Brian, in the meantime, had gone back to London and decided to remain there.

On Sunday, August 27, he was found dead in his bedroom. A coroner pronounced his death as accidental, due to the cumulative effect of bromide in a drug known as Carbitol. Brian had been taking this for some time, because of perpetual trouble with insomnia.

Within a few days, it was announced that his brother, Clive, had been appointed the new chairman of Nems Enterprises. The Beatles decided they would manage their own business affairs. Their statement to this effect was the inauguration of their decline.

CHAPTER FIVE

Seeds of Apple

Brian Epstein's death was an untimely inconvenience for the Maharishi Mahesh Yogi. With such celebrated personalities as the Beatles, Mick Jagger and Marianne Faithfull snatching at the pearls that tumbled from his lips, His Holiness had managed to monopolize the British headlines for two days. A vast brigade of journalists brandishing their steno-pads had invaded his summer conference at Bangor, Wales. Maharishi was obviously relishing the publicity. Then the news of Brian's death reached Bangor. The guru brought his greater wisdom to bear upon the situation. He advised the Beatles to smile because it wasn't important. The leaders of a generation obediently followed his bidding.

"Our meditations have given us the confidence to stand such a shock," John Lennon told reporters.

Confidence was one thing, ability was quite another. Two days of meditation wasn't enough, as their next venture proved.

Paul McCartney, industrious as ever, decided he would give the group a new direction. For some time, Paul had been stepping up his role as sole, self-appointed navigator of the Beatles' artistic development. He persuaded the others they should go ahead and make *Magical Mystery Tour,* the concept for a film with which they'd been vacillating for some time. Paul would write, inspire, direct, arrange and generally take charge of everything. He even tried to find time to knock Nems Enterprises into shape, says the company's then newly appointed chairman, Clive Epstein. Unfortunately, McCartney failed to realize that the Beatles' invisible protection was gone. During the next few months, his efforts were frustrated time and again. Several friends say he developed a lot of retrospective regard for Brian Epstein in view of this. Certainly, the *Mystery Tour* showed a dismal lack of organization and direction.

"We went out to make a film and nobody had the vaguest idea of what it was all about," says Neil Aspinall. "There were these incredible scenes dashing about the West of England with a busload of actors. We didn't know any of them and they were forever complaining that they wouldn't share a room with somebody or other. We went all the way to Brighton, yet when we got there, we ended up filming two cripples on the beach. What we should have been filming, if anything, was all the confusion, because that was the *real* mystery tour. We should have filmed John Lennon ripping the damn signs off the bus to stop people following us. We should have filmed the carloads of reporters trailing around after us, or the chaotic traffic jams we caused, whenever the bus got stuck. The problem was that with Brian dead, there was nobody to organize anything. Before he died, you'd ask for twenty cars and fifteen hotel rooms and it would all be taken care of."

Magical Mystery Tour was shown on British TV over Christmas 1967. The critics pounced on it like hungry jackals, chewed it up and spat out the remnants as "contemptuous nonsense" and "blatant rubbish." Paul McCartney pleaded lack of understanding.

"We thought we would not underestimate people and would do something new," he wailed. But the vast majority of the twenty million viewers were unsympathetic. As far as they were concerned, *Magical Mystery Tour* was a monumental, first failure.

The Beatles retreated to India to confer once again with the Charles Atlas of the spiritual teachers. Meditation, Maharishi-style, turned out to be very undemanding, consuming only half an hour a day. The Beatles had plenty of time to write a new batch of songs for their next album. But disillusionment soon set in. Rumors reached their ears that Maharishi, not attending entirely to spiritual matters, had taken a fancy to Mia Farrow. That settled it. John Lennon took on the duty of calling the Maharishi to task. He bluntly told His Holiness that the Beatles' interest in spiritual regeneration had been terminated. They were leaving for London. The venerable guru was distressed, but he didn't creep back into his expensive bungalow. Instead, he flew to New York, hired himself no less a public relations firm than Solters and Sabinson and installed himself at the Plaza, coincidentally the first New York hotel to accommodate the Beatles. Evidently, he had gained in secular experience from them.

But the Beatles had learned nothing from their bitter experience with Maharishi. They felt they'd been made to look fools. Back in London, they gave their attention to a more serious enterprise, their new two-million-dollar business venture, Apple. Apple was to manage the Beatles' partnership, under terms laid down in a deed signed by the Beatles in April 1967. This renewed their earlier partnership, Beatles Ltd. The new terms were very specific, but it seems they were either forgotten or ignored until four years later, when an English judge referred to them as an important consideration in his decision to appoint a receiver to manage the partnership assets. Lennon claims he can't even remember signing the document.

Apple's London headquarters today is a white Georgian townhouse located among the sleek tailoring establishments of Savile Row. Its elegant features have been shrouded for more than a year in a mass of scaffolding, apparently necessary for the construction of a recording studio in the basement. To get to the reception desk, it is necessary to step through a pile of sandbags. An attractive blonde behind the desk raises her eyes very reluctantly from her magazine to see who's arrived to bother her. The girl lets the phone ring six or seven times. Then she interrupts her flirtation with two loafers.

"Hello . . . well, I can't help you . . . no, because I'm not the receptionist, she's out to lunch . . . me, I'm the cook . . . 'bye!"

Enter four very young, very nervous tourists, who hesitate to step on the bourgeois, olive carpet, recognizing that this particular color may have been the personal choice of one of their heroes. Rows of framed Beatle LPs on the walls only contribute to their trepidations. The receptionist-cook pushes a pile of cheap publicity photos across the desk toward them and resumes her flirtation with the loafers. Meekly, each youngster takes a picture, gawps at it adoringly and backs out of the room.

Aside from the unorthodox style of Apple's receptionists, there isn't much to interest or amuse a visitor to the Savile Row office these days. Neil Aspinall now occupies the Beatles' old office with its Regency ceiling, brick fireplace and old worn furniture. He shuffles through a pile of magazines, turns up the $20,000 worth of checks he has been looking for, chuckles at a *Screw* Magazine article on Linda Eastman, then sets it aside with a sigh to begin reminiscing. Apart from him, the place seems to have filled up with qualified accountants. Apple will never exactly hum with quiet efficiency, but the atmosphere is markedly different from the halcyon days of 1968. That was an era when anarchists had virtually taken over, before a new regime swept them all aside.

John Donbar can't recall who first mentioned Apple, but he claims the rather questionable credit for his own apartment as the birthplace of the idea. Paul decided that the company should be the Beatles' foundation for underprivileged artists, though not all the motives for setting it up were as philanthropic. At this time, the Beatles didn't mind Nems Enterprises taking a quarter of their record royalties. They just didn't want any gray-suited accountant telling them how to handle their creative inspirations. Now Brian was dead, there was nobody they respected at Nems, and it seemed illogical that a complete outsider should get his paws in the pot of gold. Apple was to be their own plaything. The only suggestion they accepted was that unless a certain amount of their money was spent, they would be faced with that ominous figure, the British taxman, standing cap-in-hand before their door. It was a piece of advice that they heeded to the full. The Beatles certainly knew how to spend money.

Apple's two million dollars would be invested through five divisions, electronics, films, publishing, records and retailing. The company would discover new talent, assist struggling artists and market inventions. Offers of financial assistance went to people with all sorts of utterly impractical ideas, and as a result, Apple became a magnet for dreamers. Some of the dreamers, however, were really hungry.

Among those with the most voracious appetite for Beatle money was a group of three young Dutch clothing designers. Simon Posthuma claimed he was a leader in avant-garde art in Holland. With two female companions, Josje Leeger and Marijke Koger, he'd converted a barber's shop in Amsterdam into a boutique called "The Trend." A lot of clothes were sold, but as often happened with these three people, their overhead increased dramatically. When the arduous task of accounting finally began, they discovered that all profit had been wiped out. Their beautiful venture was shuttered and they took to the road.

Simon and Marijke drifted around various European capitals, eventually winding up in London. There, they met two publicists working for Brian Epstein's Saville Theater, Simon Hayes and Barry Finch. The Dutch designers were invited to produce some ostentatious stage costumes and evidently impressed Hayes and Finch with their work. Their former partner, Josje, joined them in London and Barry Finch soon left his job in publicity, bringing the design team to four. Hayes became their business manager.

At this time, the Beatles were caught up with color and psychedelia, working on a TV special, "All You Need Is Love." The design team, who by now called themselves "The Fool," produced the costumes for the show. The clothes were a success. The Fool had established themselves with the Beatles. George Harrison asked them to design a fireplace for his bungalow and John Lennon wanted a piano painted at his house in Weybridge. The Fool sniffed money. They approached the Beatles about cooperating on a boutique venture. As Neil Aspinall put it: "They crept up on us." The Beatles had been giving some thought to opening a chain of retail stores. They agreed to back the idea of a novel store with up to $250,000. One former Apple employee says they even consented to find The Fool somewhere to live.

The Beatles selected a store on Baker Street and The Fool set to work. They insisted that the exterior of the store be coordinated with the interior. With their usual carefree attitude to expense, the designers hired about thirty art students to do the strenuous work of painting the building. Everything in the store would be for sale, clothes, furniture, *objets d'art,* even the ash trays. The shop was supposed to offer something for everybody. Unfortunately, it offered nothing more than any other boutique, except perhaps to its employees. One girl, who worked in the store, admitted she used to fiddle about one hundred fifty dollars a week, the same as many others, she said. But the Beatles' problems with their staff were minor in comparison to the duress caused by The Fool and their business manager, Simon Hayes.

Hayes had worked for Brian Sommerville, one of the Beatles' first publicists, before he was employed by Brian Epstein. His publicity firm, Mayfair Public Relations, folded when Epstein died. Hayes even admitted in one of his biography handouts that it was Brian's money that had kept his PR firm stable. His explanation for the deterioration in relations between The Fool and the Beatles was that chaos had set in at Apple, and nobody knew how to run a business. He claimed The Fool were getting the rough end of the deal and were "slowly being squeezed out of money." "After three months of trying to get it to-

gether," he managed to get them released from their
contract with Apple and made a deal with Mercury Records' president, Irving Green, to bring them to the United
States. He then turned over their management to his old
partner at Mayfair, Ben Stagg, while he became a product
director for Mercury.

Correspondence passing between Apple and The Fool
tells a slightly different story. As early as January 1968,
the head of Apple's wholesale division wrote to The Fool
stressing that "there may be no expenditure of any kind"
of company resources without written authority. The following month, John Lyndon, head of Apple Retail, wrote
to The Fool, claiming that the design group had "a considerable amount of items as yet unpaid." By March,
Lyndon's patience was evidently exhausted. He wrote to
The Fool's manager, informing him that if any more gar-
ments were taken from Canel's work room, he would
have no alternative but to exclude the group from the
premises.

The Fool, however, had secured their immediate future
elsewhere. Mercury Records' president, Irving Green, had
been so impressed with them that he asked his son-in-
law, New York attorney Sanford Ross, to handle legal
details on their behalf, in order to protect their name and
designs in the United States. Ross wrote a letter to The
Fool which brought joy to their hearts. Green was advancing all costs incurred. The Fool were no fools. When the
Apple juice ran dry, they struck another well at Mercury
Records and Simon Hayes lost no time replying to Ross's
letter.

But The Fool were not finished with Apple yet. Two
more months went by before their ways parted. "Then
they crept out as they had crept in," said Neil Aspinall.
One Apple employee compared The Fool's spending to
that of drunken sailors. "No punitive action was threatened because the Beatles were so embarrassed," she recalled. They wanted nothing more to do with the boutique
business. In July, all the shop's employees were given two
weeks' notice. The remaining stock would be given away,
a gesture that wasn't quite as magnanimous as it seemed.
Apple employees all remember the evening before the

big giveaway. The Beatles, skillfully commandeered by Yoko Ono, descended on the store and seized all the best clothes. The following day about $35,000 worth of stock was pillaged by the public.

Meanwhile, The Fool were warming up to give Mercury Records a run for their money in recording costs. Many letters from Mercury's executives to Simon Hayes, now keeping a watchful eye over the recording of The Fool's first album, had a similar tone to those Hayes received from Apple. One Mercury employee involved with The Fool at this time was A&R man, Bob Reno, who had joined the company in the summer of 1969.

"The Fool insisted that all their recording be done in top secrecy," said Reno. "I was A&R director, but even I was excluded from the sessions. They said they wanted to vibrate with the engineer. I hated the group artistically. In the end, I recommended that we drop them. They cost Mercury a bundle of money. Sanford Ross once sent them a letter, telling them to cut down on telephone costs. They tore it up and sent it back to him in little pieces with a note saying, 'We don't want to hear this kind of shit.' "

Eventually The Fool completed an album for Mercury and their relationship ended there.

"I vomited when the record was released," says Bob Reno. "It was dreadful and it sold about three copies. Needless to say, the art work was gorgeous."

While The Fool's exploits were helping to bring about the downfall of Apple Retail, the company's electronics division was struggling with an even more extraordinary nonproducer, a hip Hellenic acquaintance of Lennon's, whom he had once described as "the original mad inventor." Alexis Mardas, a/k/a "Magic Alex," had been introduced to Lennon by John Donbar. "He went to John when he couldn't get any more money or interest from me for his crazy schemes," says Donbar. The Beatles set up Alex in a laboratory and backed him with funds, estimated by Derek Taylor to have run to tens of thousands of pounds. Alex's first task was to rig up lighting and sounds in the Apple boutique, a comparatively humble exploit for so reputedly talented an inventor. Then, he went to work on more complex schemes. Aspinall says he and the Beatles were most impressed with a Magic Alex contraption, producing sound from a record player through a transistor radio without the use of any wiring.

"We sat down at a dinner table and Alex put a transistor radio on the table," Aspinall remembers. "The radio was playing 'I Wanna Hold Your Hand,' and at first we thought it was a song on the radio. Then we realized that the sound was coming from a record player through the transistor."

Alex didn't need to convince the Beatles that his gadgets had some practical value. He brought them an electric apple which pulsated light and music and a "nothing-box" which had twelve lights, ran for five years, and, as its name suggests, did exactly nothing. The Beatles were mightily impressed and turned out their wallets. None of the devices produced by Alex for Apple ever reached the marketplace. The patents lie in a drawer at the London office, waiting for Allen Klein to decide what to do with them.

The funding of Alex only accelerated the tremendous spending of Beatle money already underway. As soon as the first Apple office was opened on Wigmore Street, the hangers-on ushered themselves through the door on the Beatles' coattails. The Beatles failed to realize just how many leeches had installed themselves. By the time John and Paul arrived in New York in the spring of 1968 to announce Apple to the United States, hungry mouths were already consuming Beatle whisky and driving Beatle cars. Even the announcement of Apple itself did not go as planned. The two Beatles intended to outline their reasons for its formation, but with the help of an unprepared interviewer, Joe Garagiola, they succeeded only in informing thirty million viewers that they had money to give away. Pan American and TWA must still be wondering why their flights to London were so fully booked the next day.

Many former Apple employees retain vivid memories of their employment with the Beatles. The scenes they describe suggest that the Beatles offered eleven months' paid vacation after one month's work. As one employee put it: "If you wanted a drink, you just went to Derek

Taylor's office. There were always two or three journalists in there bombed out of their minds. But not to score. For that you went to the office boy." Many of the strollers of the record and film industries rated the Savile Row office higher than any St. James' club, so lavish was the refreshment and entertainment. This was more like *Satyricon* than the road shows could ever have been. Half-empty glasses of Scotch lay about the place, telephones went unanswered, and parties, which at first began only after hours, became a regular feature of the afternoons. Some girls working at Apple had previously been employed by Nems. They were introduced to a new way of running a business.

Chris O'Dell started work at Apple early in 1968. When she told the girls from Nems that she'd attended several Beatle recording sessions, they were amazed. Brian Epstein would never have let that happen, they told her.

Of all the Beatles, she thought Paul was the most organized.

"He used to come to the office at 9:30 to make sure everybody was there by ten," she said. "He'd stay there all day and he'd go around checking on things, little weird things, like was there toilet paper in the bathrooms.

"At first, the Beatles held regular meetings with all their staff. They all came to the first one, then only two or three would come and finally just Paul. He, at least, was competent. When they decided to close the shop, he called everybody into his office to tell them exactly what was happening.

"John and Yoko had an office, but they never seemed to do much. When Allen Klein showed up, all four Beatles attended one of his first meetings with them. John fell asleep on the couch once. At the end, they woke him up and told him he'd missed the whole thing. But he hadn't. He'd had a tape recorder going all the time.

"The Beatles thought facts and figures weren't important. They didn't even want the accounts department to be in the Savile Row building. They said, 'Let's put it somewhere else because we don't want to bother about that!' They wanted the place to be full of personalities like Derek Taylor, who played the role of court jester."

Chris O'Dell described Taylor's function at Apple as "a publicist who did little or no publicity," because he was always concerned with the Beatles. His main job was to keep them happy. Other Apple observers have noted, less kindly, that Taylor spent a considerable amount of time staring at nodding toy birds floating in a tray of water in his office and making frequent comments about the greenness of their beaks.

Taylor remembers the Apple heydays as a continual series of frustrations, yet he regrets their passing.

"I'm sad and sorry that Lennon feels the way he does about the past because I certainly don't feel that way about it," he emphasizes. "He felt desperate, well they all did, about not being able to find somebody to replace Brian when they were in a mess, but they'd filled the place up with all these old courtiers from Liverpool. Although the situation wasn't good, there was still money coming into Apple; it was just that so much was being spent on things that would never bring in any return, such as whisky.

"The main problem was that the Beatles are such stubborn people. They didn't want to be ordinary businessmen, and in their position they had trouble finding new liaisons, so in came their old friends. The feelings of people at Apple toward them when they started quarreling were very strange. It was like children watching their parents quarrel and not being able to understand it. I mean, I thought they were saviors, so did a lot of people, but we overestimated them. They're just ordinary human beings.

"When Apple started they had dreams of changing things. Some of the people they brought in were very competent. Peter Asher was running A&R. He turned up with James Taylor, but James didn't get anywhere with Apple. [Taylor's record sold only a few thousand copies.] Asher worked very hard and he didn't throw either his weight or the Beatles' money around. Another good worker was Neil Aspinall, who will be at Apple until the cows come home. Had he been left alone to run it, he might have done a fine job, but the Beatles consistently interfered. It was impossible to get a decision that they all agreed on. Sometimes, you couldn't even get a majority. They were already disagreeing musically among themselves, especially over which artists they were to record.

"Some of the divisions at Apple functioned, others didn't. The film division never made any successful films, except *Let It Be,* and the retail division was always a mess. The closing of the shop was their first real shock. After the summer of 1967, with all that good weather and good acid, they opened a store while this feeling was still in existence. As soon as the summer was over, the shop didn't make sense.

"They were very quickly bored with business. After the announcement on the American TV show, the invasion started and they were soon disillusioned. They had wanted to help everybody, but the Beatles in one building could not supply what everybody wanted, and everybody, it seemed, wanted something. I would spend ten hours a day just trying to please, just so people would at least go away feeling that they'd been received, even though they got nothing."

On many occasions, those with nothing to offer walked out of Apple with something, whereas often when somebody talented did appear, he failed to obtain a royal audience. James Taylor was among the first new talents the Beatles were to develop, but after a short while they paid little attention to him. After all, where did this skinny kid rank in the pop hierarchy in comparison with them? Paul McCartney was more concerned with his harebrained scheme to ensure that the world would be wearing "demob" suits in a year's time, while Lennon was generously doling out thousands of dollars to support children's puppet shows on Brighton beach.

Between the Beatles and their employees, it was a kind of dual rape. Many members of the staff robbed them left and right, but the Beatles flattered, magnetized, seduced and finally abandoned many who worked for them. The old buddies from Liverpool spent most of their time patting Beatle backs and taking every opportunity to hack off a piece of the empire for themselves. Their attitude to any newcomer was: "We're closer to them than you, so watch it." For a while the Beatles remained aloof from petty office politics. Smiling and unquestioning, they appeared like sheiks sitting fatly on newly acquired wealth They continued to postpone their board meetings and, on the rare occasions that these were held, based their business decisions on the readings of the *I Ching*. Then slowly, they began to dabble in the mess themselves. Finally, they went searching for an exterminator to rid them of the locusts.

The most conscientious and frustrated man at Apple was Neil Aspinall. He had been asked to act as managing director while the Beatles were in India. As things turned out, he battled for longer than he expected with an ever-deteriorating situation.

"After Brian died, there was nobody to deal with the likes of Dick James [the Beatles' music publisher]," he says. "I had to be here to take calls from such people. I always had to get the Beatles' approval, but they were never able to agree. They were forever throwing out each other's ideas. Nobody will ever know just how much money was spent, because everything was in such chaos. Some accounts were kept, but not at all levels."

Apple's first accounts finally materialized in the spring of 1970. Among other items, the accountants wrote off three motor vehicles, purchased by the company, because they were unable to verify their ownership, or even their physical existence. Also written off were advances of $4,800 to John Donbar and $2,400 to Alexis Mardas, both made through Apple's electronics division. The latter amount, the accountants believed, was donated for the purchase of yet another motor car. Of course, these accounts only covered the period to the end of 1967, well before Apple entered its heyday.

It was a painful decline for the four dilettantes. Before Brian Epstein's death, they had easily slid into anything to which they turned their hands. Brian, they always said, had done nothing; now doubts were beginning to enter their minds. The pressures of business were on their own shoulders, and inevitably, their artistry began to suffer. They lacked any purpose or direction. They drove to the Apple office in Rolls-Royces, haggled with each other about the relative merits of their various protégés and watched old friends living like Romans under Nero at their expense. The employees took sides in their arguments and this only contributed to the disintegration. The Beatles drifted from one idea to another, showing a spark of enthusiasm for one venture, then quickly losing interest in favor of the next. They were quite involved with *Yellow Submarine* for a short while, but long before it was completed, its producer was having trouble obtaining their cooperation.

Before Brian Epstein died, he had met with American film producer, Al Brodax, and agreed to the production of a cartoon feature film. Both the Beatles and Brian treated it as a throwaway, a means of fulfilling their obligation to provide United Artists with a third film. Brodax, a classic, opinionated Manhattanite, had leaped on the Beatle bandwagon two years earlier with a thirty-nine-episode Beatles cartoon series for ABC TV. He pestered Epstein with his proposal for the cartoon feature, until the Beatles' manager agreed to meet him in London. Even then, Epstein, wary by this time of high-powered Beatlemongers, tried to wriggle out of his lunch appointment with Brodax, but fortunately for the film producer Epstein's personal assistant, Wendy Moger, locked Brian in his office, making sure that he would be available for the meeting.

Brodax eventually obtained a "yes" from the man he regarded as a "brilliant but very miserable son-of-a-bitch." He dashed off to New Hampshire and co-wrote the screenplay with Erich Segal, who received $16,000 for his efforts, and as Brodax points out, went on to achieve several astounding failures before he came up with *Love Story*. *Yellow Submarine* was halfway completed when the Beatles dropped by the London studio, shortly after their return from India. Brodax was keen to have them appear in the movie, and after seeing the cartoons they agreed to appear live in the last scene. Brodax hadn't intended to use their real voices at all. He'd found four boys with strong Liverpool accents to fulfill those particular roles. They turned out to be the physical opposites of the Beatles. Ringo's interlocutor was a strapping, corpulent figure, Paul's was ugly and dwarfish. But Brodax was delighted

Paul and Linda throw a party at the Empire Ballroom in London to introduce their new group "Wings." Jes' plain folks.

Brian Epstein listens to the Beatles rehearsing "All You Need Is Love."

John and Yoko, spending time away from their luxury hotel suite in New York to protest highway construction through an Indian reservation.

Photo by United Press International

George Harrison and Ravi Shankar announce their plans for the Bangladesh charity concert.

Photo by United Press International

Ringo Starr with his wife Maureen.

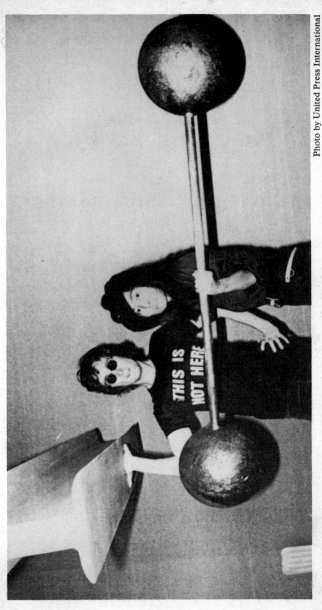

John and Yoko, putting their strong-arm techniques to the test at Yoko's one-man art show in Syracuse, New York.

John Eastman, always at McCartney's shoulder during the business and legal disputes.

Allen Klein, the toughest wheeler-dealer in the pop-music business. He won three Beatles to the Eastmans' one.

EMI chairman, Sir Joseph Lockwood. The Beatles' business tangles caused him plenty of headaches.

ATV boss, Sir Lew Grade. He couldn't obtain the Gershwin song rights, but he won the Beatles'.

John Lennon's psychedelic Rolls-Royce. It now resides in Allen Klein's garage.

A psychedelic home—George Harrison's bungalow in Esher. Later, the Beatle who warned "Beware of Maya" forsook the bungalow for a mansion.

The Fool's mural on the wall of the Beatles' Apple shop in London's Baker Street. More Beatle money down the drain.

Photo by United Press International (UK) Ltd., London

Paul McCartney with former girl friend, actress Jane Asher. A relationship that wasn't to last.

Photo by United Press International

George Harrison and his wife Patti arrive at court to appear on a charge of marijuana possession.

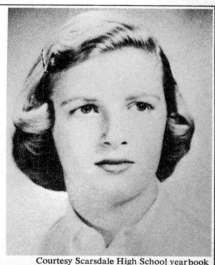

LINDA L. EASTMAN
Advertising Club 4;
Chorus 1, 2, 3, 4;
Pep Club 3, 4.
"Strawberry Blonde"
....Yen for men
....Shetlandish.

Courtesy Scarsdale High School yearbook

Brian Epstein receives an award from Princess Margaret on behalf of the Beatles.

Brian Epstein arrives in New York to sort out the John Lennon–
Jesus Christ incident. With him is Nat Weiss.
"What will it cost to cancel the tour?"
"A million dollars."

Jackson, Mississippi, teenagers burn Beatle records after news reaches the Bible belt of Lennon's comments about the relative popularity of the Beatles and Jesus.

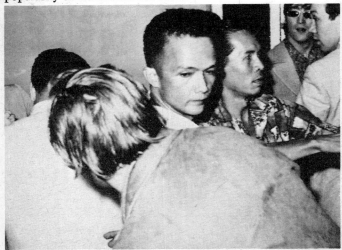

Filipinos, angered by an alleged snub of the Philippines' first lady, rough up the Beatles at Manila Airport. Ringo ducks in the foreground.

Allen Klein. His ability to sniff out pop-music money has made him a widely feared man in the record industry.

Allen Klein, George Harrison and Ravi Shankar hold a press conference to announce the Bangladesh concert.

George Harrison, Bob Dylan and Leon Russell at the charity concert for Bangladesh refugees in Madison Square Garden.

when they not only agreed to appear, but even offered to write some songs for the film.

Brodax' delight at having the Beatles participate was short-lived. Apple began to occupy their attentions and they had little time for the cartoon feature. The songwriting for *Yellow Submarine* was a last-minute effort. At two o'clock in the morning in E.M.I.'s studio, with the London Symphony Orchestra waiting patiently to go home, Brodax and *Yellow Submarine* were still one song short. George Harrison told the film producer to sit tight, while he knocked out another tune. After an hour or two, he returned to the studio with the final song. "Here Al," he said. "It's only a Northern Song."

Brodax does not retain too fond a memory of his associations with the Beatles. Paul McCartney, he felt, was a "wise-ass kind of a guy," while he described Ringo as a "clutz," who turned up one day at the studio stoned and spent the entire time walking 'round and 'round, until eventually he prostrated himself by tripping over a glockenspiel. The resounding clang was kept in the soundtrack. Brodax also had to contend with a new member of the Beatle entourage, a woman who he says tended to try and run things and order people around: the inimitable Yoko Ono.

A few months earlier, John Lennon had visited the Indica art gallery, run by his friend, John Donbar. He had taken particular interest in one art show. Among its exhibits was a ladder leading to a painting which hung from the ceiling. John climbed the ladder, picked up a magnifying glass dangling from a chain and read the tiny lettering on the canvas. It read "yes." Lennon wanted to meet the artist and Donbar introduced him to Yoko. She handed him a card which read "breathe." Lennon panted.

Lennon's first wife was a shy, local girl, who was content to remain quietly at home while he and his pals conquered the world. For a long time this suited John, a chauvinist of the first degree until he read about women's liberation in the *Village Voice* and discovered a new cause. Yoko was able to give him an intellectual tussle, which he had previously experienced only from other men. With Yoko ever present, Paul McCartney's reign as Lennon's princess was doomed.

"I don't know how it happened," said John. "I just realized that she knew everything I knew, and more probably, and that it was coming out of a woman's head. It just sort of bowled me over. It was like finding gold or something, to find somebody that you could go and get pissed with, and have exactly the same relationship as any mate in Liverpool you'd ever had. But you could go to bed with it, and it could stroke your head when you felt tired, or sick or depressed. It could also be mother.

"As she was talking to me I would get high, and the discussion would get to such a level that I would be goin' higher and higher. When she'd leave I'd go back to this sort of suburbia. Then I'd meet her again and me head would go open like I was on an acid trip."

Yoko Ono's conservative family moved from Japan to the United States when she was nineteen. For the most part, her parents remained aloof from their children. Yoko used to make an appointment if she wanted to see her father. When the family settled in Scarsdale, New York, a natural breeding ground for Beatle wives, it seems, she was packed off to Sarah Lawrence, where she was nearly expelled for missing too many classes. Her truant hours were spent alone, composing in the music library. After three years she dropped out of Sarah Lawrence and married a Japanese musician, whose social credentials were insufficient to impress her parents. They cut her off financially.

The marriage broke up after seven years. Yoko rented a loft in Greenwich Village and muscled in on the New York underground art world. Eventually, she returned to Japan to stage some of her first "events." An art critic, who attended an all-night affair at the Nanzenji Temples in Kyoto, wrote that "the who's who of the Japanese art world was enticed by her and all performed and participated in her concert like a bunch of fools succumbing to the queen bee." Yoko has never taken kindly to the least criticism of her work. She tried to kill herself and spent some time in a mental hospital.

Her second husband was an American filmmaker, Tony

Cox, by whom she had a baby daughter. He became little more than her producer and most of their time together was spent arguing. For a while after she met Lennon he was merely a friend and a patron. She fascinated John with her bohemian image and seriousness about her work. He taught her about rock and she showed him around the world of nihilistic art.

"When I started tellin' Yoko about what our life was like, she couldn't believe it," said John. "She was like this silly eastern nun wanderin' about, thinkin' it was all spiritual."

The rest of the Beatles were soon to learn of the couple's togetherness. As the recording of the "White Album" began, Yoko had her bed moved into the E.M.I. studios. She wasn't confined to it though. She would follow John everywhere, says a technician who was present at the sessions, even to the men's room. Paul and George gawped and let their opinions be known, none too subtly. Yoko wanted to be one of the boys and participate with her new beau's buddies. But Liverpool men are expected to work with their mates and leave the women to take care of the cooking. John saw in Paul and George and the other male members of the Beatle entourage the male chauvinism from which he was trying to escape. He decided that Yoko and he would keep themselves to themselves. While they played together with their events, Paul played with his new company.

Yoko Ono is ready to admit that she's not an easy person to get along with. "Somebody once told me," she said, "that I don't make small talk and that's why men hate me." Others might offer different reasons. She is as arrogant as her art, as ambitious as her husband and as temperamental as Mount Fuji. When she's criticized she lashes back or storms off in a huff, not wanting to hear. From her vantage point in Allen Klein's office she screams her instructions down the telephone.

"Listen, I'm an artist and I've got my ego to satisfy, so get on with it, okay?"

John looks slightly embarrassed. The Apple staff give her the finger behind her back and mutter "bitch." The tough little prizefighter curls up in her chair and waits for the next round. As a child she went through a lot of pain. Now it's her turn to dole it out to others.

Yoko is well aware that to be a successful artist, she must also be an astute businesswoman. For the reprinting of her book, *Grapefruit,* a series of Kahlil Gibran-like exhortations with a sprinkling of humor, she ordered 2,000 pairs of nylon panties, for use as novelty wrappings for copies destined for reviewers and friends. One lady reviewer said she would have preferred the pants and just a greeting card. Yoko also sent her assistants to a New York bookstore buying up copies of the previous issue, in the hope of stimulating a demand.

Part of Yoko's petulance and driving ambition can be attributed to the trouble she's had getting her work accepted. She is deadly serious about her art. When she's not gritting her teeth with determination, a charming, exuberant smile spreads across her face. Then, she does evoke the aura of an ocean child, the meaning of her name. At other times, she appears almost demonic in her black trousers and black sweater, with her long, black flowing hair. Her eyes are usually ringed with black shadows, by-products of non-stop work.

Although alert, enlightened and resourceful, Yoko was still unrecognized and unpublished until her late twenties, a frustrated artist whose work was considered too sexy, erotic and gimmicky for the John Cage era of the fifties in New York. Now, at thirty-eight, seven years older than Lennon, she still craves acceptance from a constituency that has never quite called her to its bosom. Although many of her New York art friends have impressed Lennon, a newcomer to the city's art world, they could no longer be described as leaders of the avant-garde. Still Yoko persists.

She encouraged the exhibitionist in Lennon and Paul disapproved. John says Paul and his "henchmen" at Apple wanted to kill *Two Virgins.* He claims he gave them every chance to become accustomed to the idea that Yoko was there to stay, but they continued to be abusive to her. John was soon offending Paul's sense of middle-class respectability and as each pursued his own interests, they began to grow apart.

Paul engaged in a brief romance with Francie Schwartz, an ambitious New York girl, who, armed only with a film script, managed to by-pass the Apple infighting and snare herself a Beatle for a while. But Francie's tenure at Paul's St. John's Wood house was short-lived. She was soon dislodged by a much more determined woman and went off dejectedly to write her memoirs for *Rolling Stone*.

Linda Eastman had met Paul McCartney briefly during one of the Beatles' American tours. She didn't really catch his attention until the spring of 1967 at a party celebrating the release of "Sergeant Pepper." Her writer friend, Lillian Roxon, came across a newspaper photograph of Paul and Linda together at the party. She gave it to Linda, who blew it up and stuck it on her bathroom wall, alongside a photo of herself and Mick Jagger. She also sent Paul a picture of himself with his lips pursed, on which she had superimposed another photo of her daughter making the same expression. Antics typical of any groupie, except Linda wasn't just any groupie.

She was a well-educated, nice Jewish girl from a family affluent enough to maintain houses in Scarsdale and East Hampton, as well as an apartment on Park Avenue. Her father Lee, a strict disciplinarian, had introduced her to all the right people, taken her to openings at the Museum of Modern Art and pointed her in what he thought was the right direction. But even at Scarsdale High School, she was considered a little bit flighty. Friends say her main interest was men.

When Linda was eighteen, her mother, a very beautiful, cultured and independently wealthy lady, was killed in a plane crash. It was a great shock to her because she had adored her mother. Lee Eastman remarried soon afterward, and Linda too was soon beckoned to the altar. She moved to Denver with her husband, John See, a geologist, and the couple had a baby daughter, Heather. The marriage didn't work out as Linda would have liked, so one morning she simply packed her belongings and her daughter into a car and drove to California. Her husband went back to his rocks, but Linda involved herself with rock.

When she returned to New York, she rejected the

starched, upright values which her father had imposed on her, took up photography and became an empress among groupies. Lee Eastman, conservative, established theatrical lawyer, didn't like to see his daughter sink to the company of East Village street girls, a girl friend of Linda's recalls.

Linda worked as an assistant for *Town and Country* Magazine, but preferred press conferences for rock stars. Her friend, Lillian Roxon, was surprised to find such a "town and country" type drawn to the rock scene. Her finishing school accent might have seemed out of place at the Fillmore, but her natural assets—high cheekbones, wide, swaying hips and well-proportioned breasts—set many a rock star drooling. Although she discarded her fine clothes for T-shirts and jeans, she retained an aura of sweet-shetland. Her aristocratic presence was bestowed on the sweaty dressing rooms of innumerable rock palaces, as she marched in alone, cameras slung casually across her shoulder. She photographed Mick Jagger shortly after his breakdown. Evidently, she aided his recovery, because soon after, she wrote about her night with Mick for a teen magazine, describing how they stayed up all night phoning in requests to radio stations. *Ebony* Magazine photographed her in Harlem with Eric Burden of the Animals. Lee Eastman was furious.

Her friends say she was not a good photographer. She snapped three rolls of film of Warren Beatty without moving from her position on the floor to change the angle. The pictures were regarded as abysmal, but Linda didn't care. She'd made a hit with Beatty, if only for a short while. Linda was only temporarily distraught when a star wanted to get rid of her. She would go to an ice cream parlor and consume a whole pint of Haagen-Dazs, call her friends and invite them to indulge with her. Small wonder Paul McCartney wanted her to lose fifteen pounds. Her former friends say her Castro convertible sofa always seemed to be open and covered with crumpled bed linen, as if to advertise that a "heavy" music scene figure had just left. Her daughter, Heather, learned to look after herself at an early age. The child can count

Mike Bloomfield, Stephen Stills and Al Kooper among its more illustrious babysitters.

When the Fillmore East opened in 1968, Linda became its house photographer. John Morris, who ran the hall at the time, remembers her as a "prep-school to East Coast college girl, who was getting tired of being in and out of all sorts of different beds.

"She mothered Big Brother and the Holding Company and became close friends with Country Joe," says Morris. "But she was often depressed and I think she was desperately seeking security."

By the time John and Paul came to New York in May 1968 to announce Apple, Linda was a leading figure in the city's rock scene. At the press party she told Lillian Roxon she thought Paul was smiling at her. "What shall I do?" she asked. Lillian came up with a not-too-original suggestion, but it worked. She advised Linda to slip Paul a piece of paper with her phone number. Paul called her that night.

"Until then, Paul had never responded hugely to her," says Lillian. "In fact, she really preferred John. She used to say John is very exciting."

That night John and Paul stayed at Nat Weiss's apartment and Linda stayed with them. She went with them to the airport the next day.

"I knew Linda from 1966, when she was already the black sheep of her family," says Weiss. "At that time, she was staying with Stevie Winwood when Traffic was being formed. She used to say everything was 'groovy.' She was very capable and she loved money. There was nothing subtle about her. Paul had been through a brief romance with Francie Schwartz, who had a lot of suggestions about how to run Apple. I advised Linda to go after him. She said, 'I'm going to England, but I'm not going to sleep with Paul.' Well, needless to say. . . . The worst thing was that once she was married she turned against everybody, neglecting all her old friends."

When Paul stayed at a Beverly Hills bungalow a few weeks later, he called Linda and she flew to California. She was still not too hopeful of a lasting relationship, says a friend, because of an incident that took place at a drive-in "Jack-in-the-Box."

"Paul turned to her in the car and said, 'This is you, Linda, an instant dessert, a royal cream pudding.' She wanted to know what he meant by that!"

By October 1968, Linda was driving poor Lillian crazy because she couldn't decide whether to go and see Paul in London. Again Lillian came to her rescue. She advised Linda to invent a photographic assignment. Linda took off, never to return alone.

"Linda's not the sort of person to take second or third place in anything," says Lillian. "When she moved in I knew that was it. I still have a lot of love for her, although she was exasperating at times. She was very beautiful and sexy. Paul was very infatuated with this image of a girl on a horse, a father with a huge art collection and a Park Avenue apartment."

Linda's turnabout on her friends, once she'd installed herself with McCartney, included a total rejection of Lillian. Her former ally was very depressed and plunged into writing a rock encyclopedia. The future Mrs. McCartney became a much stronger personality. An Apple employee recalls that the company's chauffeur spent a lot of time running errands for her. She would send him back to the shop because he'd come back with half a pound of cheese when she only wanted a quarter. She made a point of telling George's and Ringo's wives that they were far too lenient with their servants.

Her friendship with Yoko was brief.

"There was a nice quality about her," says Yoko. "As a woman, she doesn't offend you because she doesn't come on like a coquettish bird, you know? She was all right and we were on very good terms, until Allen Klein came to visit. She said, 'Why the hell do you have to bring Allen into it?' She said very nasty things about Allen. I protected Allen each time she said something about him and since then she never speaks to me."

Paul and Linda came to New York late in 1968 and Paul did his share of babysitting. He was enchanted with Linda's child, say her friends. Linda was very pleased with her catch. She told John Morris of the Fillmore: "You'll never guess who's babysitting tonight."

Paul and Linda's friends feel they've both become markedly different personalities since they've been married.

"They've become very conservative, domestic and boring," says one friend. "They won't even smoke pot any more because they regard it as childish. Paul went through some difficult changes around the time his first solo album was released, and Linda's sisters were told not to say anything to the press. Paul has also decided his children won't go to an ordinary school, but he'll bring them up himself. They play with Bob Dylan's kids at recording sessions.

"They're motivated by money, and Linda, who I never saw play a piano in her life, has turned Paul onto bubble gum music. That's the music they like. I bet that's a shocker for many people. They're not interested in what George or John is doing."

Lillian has one explanation. "They seem to want to prove to everyone that 'we're groovy, we write songs together in bed. Can you dig it?' "

CHAPTER SIX

The Power Struggle Begins with Nems

While the Beatles wrestled with their new company, Brian Epstein's firm, Nems Enterprises, foundered in the shallows. For eighteen months, it attracted only the mild curiosity of a London merchant banker and a British film company. An unhappy substitute helmsman, Clive Epstein, failed to navigate her back into deeper waters. Within a few months, he too was preparing to abandon ship.

Brian Epstein had claimed he was worth nearly $17 million on paper. He had set up an intricate network of interlocking companies, with interests ranging from publishing to retail, from clubs to playwriting, from films to garages. His personal investments were equally complex. He even owned a quarter share in a Spanish bullfighter.

In 1966, he had turned down a twenty-million-dollar offer from an American for Nems, but this figure, as a value for the company, was way out of line now that its principal asset was dead.

Robert Stigwood, a ginger-haired Australian, had been taking charge of the day-to-day running of Nems since Epstein had made him co-managing director in January 1967. Brian wanted Stigwood to run all Nems' affairs, develop the company and ultimately have an opportunity to buy it. Then, he hoped to divorce the Beatles from Nems and spend more time with them. But as time passed, he slowly became disenchanted with Stigwood.

"Things had gone smoothly at first," explained Nat Weiss. "Stigwood was handling the Bee Gees well and developing them and then he bought in Cream. But by May, Brian felt that the elegant Australian was living in a style that was too grand, that money was being spent unnecessarily and that effective control of Nems was slipping from his hands into Stigwood's. In July, the Bee Gees went on a tour to the United States, but they weren't playing because Stigwood had rented a yacht for them. I asked him who would pay for it and he told me it would be charged to his personal account. I called Brian and said, 'Robert's chartered a yacht for the Bee Gees and he's charging it to his personal account.' 'The Bee Gees can charter a yacht when they've earned a million dollars,' said Brian. 'Until then they should be out playing.' So Brian was looking for a way to ease Stigwood out.

"He was also having problems with others, who, he felt, were becoming a little too lavish on the expense account. He was cracking down all 'round when he died. Then the vultures pounced. Within hours after Brian died, Peter Brown, his assistant, whom he'd brought from nowhere, was making sure the Beatles knew that it was he who would be managing them. There were innumerable meetings held in Brian's office. It was a distasteful sight to witness. Brown went on to serve Allen Klein, eventually with the same devotion."

Four days after Brian's death, his impeccably dressed and well-mannered younger brother, Clive, was appointed Nems' new chairman. Paul McCartney once described him, somewhat scornfully, as a "provincial furniture salesman." In some ways the remark was justified. As head of the Nems' entertainment complex, he appeared as a roller skater among a herd of rhinos. Within a few months, the struggle of managing the company had exhausted him and he confided to friends that all he wanted was time to relax and a chance to concentrate on his furniture business. Today, he does exactly this. In his mother's apartment in Liverpool, he explained his feelings about running Nems.

"I never really felt that Nems could continue as it was, once Brian died, because we had nobody with Brian's imagination, except possibly Stigwood, and between Stigwood and the Beatles there was quite a clash. They just didn't like him. I was little more than a caretaker for the next eighteen months."

"A very good caretaker," his mother, Queenie, interposed reassuringly.

"Brian hadn't much time for business for some months before he died," Clive continued. "I felt there was a lot of tidying up to be done. At first, the Beatles were keen to support Nems, especially Paul, but they wanted to expand rapidly and use Nems to launch their own business ideas. I wanted to get things more organized before we moved ahead. The Beatles wanted to give a break to a lot of lesser lights. In retrospect, I suspect we would have become a little Apple."

Before long, there were wide differences of opinion between Clive Epstein, Nems' other directors and the Beatles over how Nems should be managed. Clive is meticulous, pays great attention to detail and spends an inordinate amount of time checking his watch. Nat Weiss remarked that it was hardly surprising that the disputes couldn't be resolved.

"Clive developed the incredible theory that the less the company did, the more money it made," said Weiss. "He paid no attention to servicing the Beatles. They were anxious to expand, of course, and take a greater hand in managing their own affairs. They felt they were being shortchanged and they wanted nothing to do with Stigwood. Nor did Clive Epstein, who, like Brian, felt that Stigwood was too hasty when it came to spending money."

Within two months Clive Epstein and Robert Stigwood had parted company. Stigwood took with him the Bee Gees and Cream, linked up with the Grammophon-Philips record group and formed his own organization, named, naturally, after himself. He now resides elegantly one floor below Allen Klein's office in New York. He left behind a very plush office and a few tarnished Beatles' gold records. The British press attributed the disagreements between Epstein and Stigwood to a different viewpoint on international expansion. According to Weiss, Epstein was more concerned about certain items of underwear he had found charged to Nems' expense account.

In any event, Epstein was soon to change his view about international expansion. A group reorganization was announced and a new company, Nemperor Holdings, was formed to act as the parent company to Nems. Clive announced that this inaugurated a period of "vigorous domestic and international expansion" for Nems. He even appointed a new managing director, Vic Lewis, who was never exactly close friends with Brian. Apart from setting up a theatrical division and negotiating to represent a Beverly Hills agency in Britain, Nem's planned expansion didn't materialize. It continued to act as the Beatles' agent, taking a twenty-five percent cut of their record royalties, but the Beatles did not regard either Clive or Queenie Epstein, now the majority shareholder, with the apprehension and suspicion which they reserved for other businessmen. The Epsteins were not outsiders. They were part of the original Liverpool complex, if not the close friends, such as surrounded and milked the Beatles at Apple. But Nems without Brian was unable to provide the professional managerial skills demanded by the Beatles' evolving artistry. Nobody was capable of making decisions for the Beatles.

"When Brian was alive, you would ask for a decision about any Beatles-related matter, and you'd have a 'yes' or a 'no' immediately," says Nat Weiss. "Afterward, it was like the French governments of the thirties. So and so always had to speak to so and so first."

The real shock came when the filming of the *Mystery Tour* was completed.

"We didn't know who to give it to, so we gave it to Nems," said Neil Aspinall. "It was like screening it for NBC, CBS, and ABC all at once and hearing them all say they didn't like it. Where do you take it after that? Nems was in total chaos with Stigwood gone and the death taxes problem to be solved.

"The film was made in color for theaters, yet it wound up on British TV in black and white. There was nobody to make the artistic and career judgment as to whether it was good or bad, or to decide whether we should go with it or not. I'm sure Brian would have been quite capable of saying: 'Oh, so we blew twenty thousand quid, so what?' "

By the time *Magical Mystery Tour* was shown, Clive Epstein was tiring of Nems. He disliked commuting to London for board meetings. When Triumph Investment Trust, a hardheaded merchant banking firm, made a gentle overture to him early in 1968, he was willing to talk with Triumph's managing director, Leonard Richenberg. The talks broke down shortly after they began. But Richenberg, soon to become an important figure in the Beatles' business affairs, kept a close eye on Nems. The following autumn he contacted Clive Epstein again.

Leonard Richenberg, respected Oxford professor and former economics adviser to the British Treasury, is a shrewd businessman with an uncanny instinct for mergers. Triumph Investment Trust now has quite a reputation in the City of London for aggressive takeovers. But when Triumph gobbled up Nems early in 1969, the deal created quite a stir among London's city gents. Richenberg went to great pains to explain that this was a sober financial transaction, not a "wild jaunt into show business." He even admitted to the press that his own tastes in music were very conservative. His sentiments apparently were not designed to appeal to the Beatles.

"Some of the Beatles' songs are very good," he declared. "But I think about twenty minutes of any pop music is enough."

The merchant banker was curious and interested in

Nems as soon as he heard that it might be up for sale. He knew that a major British film company had been making tentative inquiries about the show business complex, so he too made some assessments of the company.

"Some aspects of Nems were difficult to put a net value on, because nobody knew at the time just how large a record royalty E.M.I. was due to pay Nems," said Richenberg. "Nems was a cash company with a large tax liability. There was little doubt that the Epsteins were going to be slaughtered by death duties.

"I knew there was an element of risk involved. There was a drug charge pending against one of the Beatles [which one he couldn't remember] and their own company, Apple, didn't seem too prosperous at the time. My offer to Epstein was devised to circumvent the death duty liability, and in effect, it was two offers. I offered to buy Mrs. Epstein's seventy percent share in Nems outright for 620,000 pounds. I agreed to pay Clive Epstein 420,000 pounds, provided the royalties to come to Nems were not less than 350,000 pounds for two years. If there were no royalties, he would get 150,000 pounds for his twenty percent stake in the company."

It was a skillful bargain, but it didn't quite go as smoothly as planned. In January 1969, Leonard Richenberg was surprised to hear from Clive Epstein that the deal was off. Nems was to be sold to the Beatles' own company, Apple. Clive Epstein had loyally decided that in view of the close links between the Epstein family and the Beatles, they should have first option to buy Nems. It took just six weeks for the Beatles' newly acquired financial advisers, the Eastman family and Allen Klein, to send Clive scurrying back to the waiting, extended arms of Leonard Richenberg.

The prelude to this turn of events had taken place in New York a few months earlier. Paul McCartney's new girl friend, Linda Eastman, had introduced her biggest catch yet to her father Lee and brother John, partners in the New York law firm, Eastman and Eastman.

"Paul had been agitating for some time for a new manager for Apple," says Nat Weiss. "He was fed up with the way the company was being run and he asked his future father-in-law, Lee, to recommend someone to put the house in order. Lee, of course, suggested his son John."

Lee Eastman was delighted with Paul's request. A business contact says that although Lee was a successful, wealthy music copyright owner and art collector, he had always wanted his name in lights. Now, here at last was his chance, a chance to represent such a prized show business phenomenon as the Beatles. His son John was dispatched to do the dirty work.

Lee had worked hard at his business. The catalogue of music copyrights he owns is most impressive, including such classics as "Never on Sunday" and "Young at Heart." After graduating from Harvard, he decided to change his name from Epstein to Eastman. In this respect, Lee Eastman provides a marked contrast to his rival, Allen Klein, who eventually won three Beatles to Eastman's one. A plaque for services to the B'nai B'rith is displayed prominently in Klein's office.

Lee Eastman's first wife, Louise, died in an air crash. She was a rich girl from a well-known Cleveland family, the Linders, owners of a large department store. Friends say she was not only the richer, but the brighter and stronger of the two, and an intense, driving force behind her husband. Lee studied hard. He became an expert in international copyright law, the best in the business, say some colleagues. But Lee's hard work didn't make him any too popular. Some of his former associates describe him as excessively overbearing and brash, though quite capable of turning on the charm when necessary. One person, who spent many years in close contact with Lee, refused to talk about him because his contempt and dislike for Lee was so great, he was afraid he might sound off too much.

But Eastman's efforts were rewarded materially. He is the owner of a fine art collection and represents some of America's great artists, Motherwell and De Kooning among others. It would certainly have pleased him to add the Beatles to the list. Whatever discussions took place at the Eastman family dining table, Paul became very interested in music publishing company shares after meeting the Eastmans. He bought several thousand shares in Northern Songs without telling the other Beatles.

"It was the first time any of us had gone behind any-one else's back," said Lennon. "When I asked Paul why he was buying these shares, he said, 'I had some beanies and I wanted some more.' "

Klein says McCartney later told him he wanted the Beatles to own Northern Songs.

Although John Eastman describes his early meetings with Paul as fairly casual, he didn't lose any time getting on a plane to London to meet the rest of the Beatles. John is an exuberant, rather excitable, young lawyer with plenty of style. In the subdued, lace-curtained elegance of his father's office with its worn leather armchairs, Matisses and Picassos, his irascibility on the telephone seems some-what inappropriate. "Oh, for Christ's sake, why's he so fuckin' smart, what does that son-of-a-bitch have?" he snaps into the receiver. With his fair, wavy hair, rep-stripe tie and cultivated Kennedy look, he epitomizes the dash-ing young executive, so prominently featured in sports car commercials. Needless to say, this image cut little ice with John Lennon, who could care less if he'd been to Stanford and N.Y.U. law school, or worked on Senator Yarborough's civil rights bill.

However, John Eastman was retained as the Beatles' general counsel and he recommended restructuring the cash flows coming into England for tax reasons. He also suggested that the Beatles buy Nems, a plan that Leonard Richenberg had not expected to have to reckon with. The Beatles agreed that this was a good idea, and fully supported Eastman in the negotiations.

"I saw Clive Epstein immediately," says Eastman. "I told him, 'Look, you can't get the money out of the com-pany to pay estate taxes, so why don't we buy Nems and you'll get the money as a capital gain.' I said, 'Forget the twenty-five percent [Nems' entitlement of Beatle rec-ord royalties]. What's the company worth? Eight hundred thousand, nine hundred thousand pounds? Forget it. We won't quibble. We'll give you a million.' "

Eastman thought the deal was done. E.M.I.'s chair-man, Sir Joseph Lockwood, had agreed to lend the Bea-tles one million pounds against future royalties, due to be handed over in a few months. Very soon, John Eastman

was on a plane back to the United States, leaving lawyers and accountants to sew up the trivial details. But
one of these details, a problem with tax warranties,
brought him tearing back to England again within a few
days.

Hot on his heels came another American contender for
the title of Beatles' manager. Brisk and businesslike New
York accountant, Allen Klein, brought with him his reputation in the pop world as a hard bargainer. Klein had
gone to great lengths to arrange a transatlantic phone call
with John Lennon after reading John's statement in the
papers that the Beatles were going broke. Through a friend
of Derek Taylor's, he had let it be known at Apple that
he wished to talk with Lennon. After several delays, he
succeeded in arranging a meeting with John and Yoko
at the Dorchester. The Beatles had been trying for several
weeks to find somebody to sort out their tangled business
affairs. Lennon wasn't confident that John Eastman could
do the job. He'd even approached Lord Beeching, the
former head of British Railways, but Beeching had turned
him down.

Both John and Yoko were extremely nervous when
they arrived at the hotel. They'd heard plenty about this
awesome figure, who managed the Rolling Stones and had
said years ago that one day he would have the Beatles.
They were surprised to find an equally nervous, bright-
eyed, stocky individual in a sweater and sneakers, alone
in his hotel room, with no assistants and no lawyers. During the course of the evening, Klein impressed Lennon
with his knowledge of the pop industry and the Beatles'
work. He knew all about their current position. Had John
Eastman taken the trouble to learn a little more about
the group, Klein might never have obtained even an audience.

"He knew all about us and our music," Lennon says of
this first encounter. "I knew right away he was the man
for us. I wrote to Sir Joseph Lockwood that night. I
said: 'Dear Sir Joe: From now on Allen Klein handles
all my stuff.'"

The next day John stomped into the Apple office and,
according to Derek Taylor, announced: "I don't give a

bugger who anybody else wants, but I'm having Allen Klein for me."

"Oh, shit!" said Linda Eastman on hearing the news. In view of subsequent events, her reaction proved quite justified.

Lennon had told Klein the night before that the Beatles were proposing to buy Nems and that John Eastman was handling the deal. Klein met with the other three Beatles the next day. He told them he couldn't recommend buying Nems, while their financial position and that of their companies remained to be ascertained. He said he was going to make inquiries into John's financial position. Ringo and George asked him to do the same. But McCartney left the meeting.

The following weekend another meeting was arranged, this time with John Eastman present, to discuss the proposed purchase. Klein says it was agreed that the idea of acquiring Nems should be shelved until he'd had an opportunity to check out the Beatles' financial state. His argument was that in order to have a million pounds to spend, you have to earn considerably more before tax. He explained that if the advance of one million pounds was to be paid back out of royalty income, then earnings of at least two million pounds would be required. John Eastman, meanwhile, was pushed to the sidelines. He agreed to act as legal adviser to the Beatles.

Before the day was out, bustling Allen met with Clive Epstein to obtain an assurance from the Nems' chairman that a decision on the disposal of Nems would be deferred for three weeks, until he'd completed his investigations. But after only two weeks, he learned from one of the Beatles' accountants that Nems had been sold to Triumph. The accountant, he said, informed him that a letter from John Eastman to Clive Epstein had sparked off the sale. He may well have been right.

On February 14, 1969, Eastman sent the following letter to Clive.*

---

* Letter submitted before the English High Court of Justice, Chancery Division, in the case of *Paul McCartney* vs. *John Lennon, George Harrison, Richard Starkey and Apple Corps Ltd.*

As you know Mr. Allen Klein is doing an audit of
the Beatles' affairs vis-à-vis Nems and Nemperor
Holdings Ltd. When this has been completed I suggest we meet to discuss the results of Mr. Klein's
audit as well as the propriety of the negotiations sur-
rounding the nine-year agreement between E.M.I.,
the Beatles and Nems.

Clive Epstein shot back a terse note.*

Before any meeting takes place, please be good
enough to let me know precisely what you mean by
the phrase "the propriety of the negotiations sur-
rounding the nine-year agreement between E.M.I.,
the Beatles and Nems."

Although Eastman claims that the note was written at
Klein's request, a claim that Klein adamantly denies, he
admits that he had taken the position that the contract
between E.M.I., the Beatles and Nems was unreasonable.
Nems would be taking twenty-five percent of their record
royalties for nine more years, even though Brian Epstein's
management contract had run out. He denies, however,
that he was responsible for the failure of the Beatles to
acquire Nems, preferring to place the blame on Allen
Klein.

"Klein was the fly in the ointment," says Eastman. "I
didn't like the man's reputation and I didn't like the way
he operated. He isn't my style. But Lennon liked him
and he talked the others into liking him. True, I wanted
Nems to assume complete liability for taxes, but that
wasn't important. Klein showed up in the meantime and
said, 'Forget it, I'll get you Nems for nothing because the
Epsteins owe you money.' It was because of Klein that
the deal fell through."

Clive Epstein disagrees. He puts the blame for the
Beatles' failure to acquire Nems squarely on John East-

---

* Letter submitted before the English High Court of Justice,
Chancery Division, in the case of *Paul McCartney* vs. *John Lennon, George Harrison, Richard Starkey and Apple Corps Ltd.*

man's shoulders, although he did admit to Nat Weiss that he was afraid of Klein.

"Eastman spent a week negotiating for Nems on the basis of the loan that Lockwood was prepared to make the Beatles," he says. "But he loaded the offer with so many conditions and warranties that he ended up talking himself out of the deal. In my opinion, he was a little too young to be negotiating at that level."

It was a bitter setback for the Beatles. They were very disappointed that the deal fell through, and even more displeased that a merchant bank would be pocketing a quarter of their royalties. They'd come very close to getting the company. Neil Aspinall, Apple's managing director, was ready to sign the check when the snags developed.

"It's fair to say that had we got Nems, a lot of our later financial problems would never have occurred," says Aspinall. "It cost the Beatles a lot more to free themselves from Triumph later. You could say the deal was crucial.

"John Eastman kept wantin' to attach these tax warranties. I kept sayin' to him, 'Shurrup, will yer,' 'cause I could see the whole deal was getting screwed up by this and that Clive didn't like the idea. If you ask me, Lee Eastman was stupid to send his son over. You tell me, would you send your son to do business with John Lennon?"

It was John Eastman's credibility that suffered with three of the Beatles when Nems was sold to Triumph. Allen Klein stood to gain.

"Eastman seemed to think that they were going to be angry with Klein," says Nat Weiss. "He flew to London thinking Klein would be ready to give up. It was like expecting Hitler to be scared off by the Liechtenstein Army. In the end, he was hoping Klein would be prepared to compromise, but Klein wasn't prepared to share out control if he could get it all. I warned Eastman that if Paul had threatened to leave then, it might still have stopped Klein. But between them all, they were like gravediggers feeding on the body of the dying."

Paul still had faith in the Eastmans. After all, they were soon to be his in-laws. He didn't like Klein from the first meeting.

113

"But he was still attracted by the Eastmans' stability and good manners," said Derek Taylor. "They have dignity and a formal approach and give the impression that they're in high places and have good connections. Paul is impressed by all that."

But all four now had to reckon with Leonard Richenberg. When Clive Epstein resumed his negotiations with Triumph, he was anxious to close the deal quickly. This suited the merchant banker because he wanted Triumph to be owners of Nems before March 31, the end of the British tax year.

"I considered what Eastman was advocating [buying Nems] to be stupid," said Richenberg haughtily. "The last thing the boys should have done was buy income. I gathered that Klein hadn't wanted the deal to go through. I still think it was a shame that the Beatles were involved with either Eastman or Klein because I think we could have harnessed their ability to do what the public wanted."

Perhaps it didn't occur to Mr. Richenberg that the Beatles neither wanted to be harnessed, nor did they want to offer what the public wanted.

"Anyway, on February 17, we were owners of seventy percent of Nemperor Holdings," said Richenberg, his eyes glittering. "Epstein was a little difficult to deal with, but I think he trusted me. In many ways he's like his brother was, good bookkeeper yes, financier no. Of course, when we did the deal there were a lot of eyebrows raised in the City. Merchant bankers buying into show business?"

Allen Klein does not take defeat easily. Within a week, he marched into Richenberg's office, accompanied by his lawyer, ready to make a deal. He wanted to find out whether Triumph was prepared to sell back the Beatles' rights invested in Nems for reasonable terms. At least that was his version. Richenberg has a different story.

The merchant banker remembers that Klein claimed large sums of money were owing to the Beatles from Nems for performances some time ago. The Beatles would be prepared to forget about this if Triumph would part with the rights to the Beatles' royalties. The tactic didn't work.

"I didn't know who he was," said Richenberg. "For all I knew he might have been a nasty little gangster. I only agreed to see him because Clive Epstein asked me to see him for Lennon's sake. He said, 'You're very smart to have jumped in first and bought Nems, but what you didn't know was that the Epsteins owed the Beatles huge sums of money from road shows.'

"Did I tell him to get lost on that first occasion? No, I put it in slightly stronger terms. Our deal with Nems was well secured with all kinds of warranties and guarantees, so I didn't see any point in continuing the discussion."

Robust, tenacious Allen Klein had met his match. Although he had evidently startled his opponent, Richenberg, or "Rikenboiger" as Klein liked to call him, would not be browbeaten. Klein called a meeting of the Beatles. They all agreed that the arrangements for Nems to collect the Beatles' royalties would be terminated. The idea that Richenberg and "the men-in-suits" should be handling their money was too abhorrent. They sent a menacing-sounding legal letter to E.M.I., demanding that their royalties be paid direct to Apple. It was signed by all four Beatles and read:

We hereby irrevocably instruct you to pay Henry Ansbacher & Co. [their own merchant banker who was not so abhorrent] all royalties payable by you directly or indirectly to Beatles and Co. or Apple Corps.

Richenberg also received a letter from the Beatles. It informed him that Nems was no longer the Beatles' agent, and that from now on their royalties from E.M.I. would be paid direct to Apple. The troubled merchant banker lost no time getting on the telephone to E.M.I.'s chairman, Sir Joseph Lockwood. The two discussed their predicament.

"Klein had realized he was getting nowhere with me and had turned his attention to Lockwood," said Richenberg. "I went to see Sir Joseph. He was being advised by Mr. Len Wood and several panicky lawyers, all scared out of their wits that the Beatles might not sing anymore, or might just sing the National Anthem backwards, if E.M.I. paid the royalties to Nems and not to Apple. I told Lockwood that our contract stated quite clearly that E.M.I. would pay the entire royalty to Nems, which was entitled to take twenty-five percent and after deducting expenses would pay the Beatles the remainder.

"Lockwood seemed willing at first to adhere to our agreement, but then he followed the advice of his lawyers. They had decided that E.M.I. was not involved, that the fight was between Nems and the Beatles. They wouldn't pay anybody until the dispute was settled. I phoned Lockwood and called him a chicken for backing down to Klein, but he'd done it anyway. Then, I commissioned a Bishop's* report on Klein, a tactic which much impressed him later, as it was the kind of move an old warrior like Klein would respect. It showed he was involved in a number of lawsuits."

Klein's strategy was neatly timed as some 1.3 million pounds of accrued royalties was due to be handed over to Nems in the next few weeks. In the meantime, he loaded his guns to prepare to get a better royalty rate for the Beatles from E.M.I. There was some dispute in the Beatles' camp about who should do the negotiating with the record company. John Eastman was anxious to attend any such meeting and Paul also wanted him to be present. Klein says it was eventually decided by all four Beatles that he alone would go to E.M.I. with them and have the authority to negotiate. They had a meeting with Lockwood in May, but the record company made it clear that it would not agree to any new terms as long as the Nems' dispute was still raging. Triumph, meanwhile, had decided to take the matter to court, requesting that the royalties be paid to them. But the judge decided that such a move was unnecessary to protect Triumph, since E.M.I. had declared it was its intention not to pay anybody and planned to ask the court for a firm ruling on the disposal of the money.

As Klein didn't seem to be progressing too well with the stubborn Richenberg, Lee Eastman decided it was

* The private detectives of big business.

time to play his cards. He arranged a meeting with the merchant banker at Claridge's, a famous London hotel, and started the discussion by ordering champagne. But Triumph's managing director wasn't so easily impressed. Eastman's offer to take Nems off Triumph's hands for one million pounds was rejected. According to Richenberg, the New York lawyer left saying: "Well, I guess we'll have to rough each other up a bit."

Richenberg did try to make contact with the Beatles directly. He offered to meet them, but not with Klein.

"I knew they were hostile to strangers owning a piece of them," he said. "But I'd made it very clear to Clive Epstein that they'd get a very good offer for their remaining ten percent share in Nems. I thought the boys were okay, but that Klein was no good, so I tried to get in touch with them. I sent each one a letter, but received no replies. I wasn't sure whether they'd been totally sold on Klein because at this time they hadn't been paid either.

"A few days before the court hearing on the royalties, Klein was on the phone wanting to settle things. We made a deal, but he backed out at the last minute and the case moved into court. It was decided that the money would be paid into the nearest branch of Lloyd's bank, pending a trial. I was satisfied with this, partly because the branch just happened to be *our* bank. Naturally, the manager was delighted with the deposit. I was also glad the money was now locked in. I thought, 'Good, we'll sit it out. I know my Klein.' "

E.M.I. hadn't wished to upset the Beatles, but neither did Leonard Richenberg. He still refused to see Klein and the Beatles together. He felt that Klein would make a proposition which he would be forced to reject. Then he would look even more like a "big, bad city financier" in the Beatles' eyes. His reason for not wishing to alienate them was that he, too, hoped to handle their business affairs.

"We didn't want to manage them," he said. "As far as I was concerned they could manage themselves. But we did hope to take care of their finances."

Richenberg too had been struck by a rather delayed attack of Beatlemania. His efforts to contact them eventually succeeded, but he took a very roundabout course. His plan involved the 1969 British finance bill.

"The bill contained a typical Labour government clause," he said. "It would have affected many groups in their position with heavy tax liabilities. I let it be known that despite our differences over Nems, I wanted to strike up a friendship with them to see if we could get the clause altered. In the end, I agreed to meet them and Klein, that Robin Hood who rarely gives to the poor."

The merchant banker moved off his own turf and ventured over to Savile Row. He sat down with the Beatles and Klein and some hard bargaining took place. His position had been strengthened by the onset of the battle for Northern Songs, the Beatles' music publishing company, in which Nems held 4.5 percent of the shares. After several meetings with Klein, whom Richenberg confesses he grew to like, a deal was hammered out. Klein's street sense and negotiating skill proved a worthy match for the clever and highly articulate Richenberg.

Triumph decided not to press its entitlement to twenty-five percent of the Beatles' royalties for the next nine years. Instead, it agreed to accept some 750,000 pounds in cash and twenty-five percent (over 300,000 pounds) of the royalties deposited following the court order. Richenberg also obtained 50,000 pounds for Nems' twenty-three percent stake in the Beatles' film company, Subafilms, as well as five percent of the Beatles' gross record royalty from 1972 to 1976. Klein had refused to budge from this figure of five percent, but Richenberg says he was satisfied with it, as he knew that Klein would soon roast E.M.I.'s chairman, Lockwood, to get the Beatles' royalty rate increased.

In return, Nems surrendered all its rights in all contracts affecting the Beatles. They received an option on the 4.5 percent of Northern Songs' shares owned by Nems, valued at 355,000 pounds. The option was for a year and the call price of thirty shillings a share was considerably lower than the market value at the time. In addition, Triumph bought the Beatles' ten percent stake in Nems for 266,000 of its own shares, valued at the time at more than 420,000 pounds.

Klein was satisfied with the deal. He had freed the Beatles from Nems and at the same time made substantial capital investments for them. "The boys will make a good profit out of it," he said.

Richenberg, too, seemed well pleased with the outcome. The Beatles were now *his* shareholders. For him the battle was over, but not for Allen Klein. There was an insurrection brewing in the Beatles' camp. The agitators were beginning to pluck up courage. Klein had obtained McCartney's signature on the agreements, but he then heard from Paul's solicitors that they had been instructed to withdraw authorization to exchange documents with Triumph until Klein and his company, ABKCO, agreed to take no fee for the negotiations and settlement.

Klein stormed across to the E.M.I. studios at Abbey Road and buttonholed Paul. He told him what had just transpired. He claims Paul replied: "That's ridiculous," and left the room.

"After a few minutes he returned," said Klein, "having evidently made a phone call. He said, 'It's all right. It's good now.' I believe he must have instructed his solicitors to agree to the exchange of documents."

Paul may have been satisfied with the settlement, but John Eastman certainly wasn't. Within a few days, the Beatles all received letters from him which read:*

Before memories become too short, I want to remind everybody that we could have settled the Nems' affairs for very little. Klein killed my deal by claiming all sorts of improper acts of Nems which his investigation would disclose, and promising to get Nems for you for nothing. We all know that no improper acts were found by Klein, if, in fact, Klein made an investigation at all.

We do know, however, that Nems tied up 1,400,-000 pounds of Beatles' phonograph recording royalties which Klein has been unable to free. Klein has

* Letter submitted before the English High Court of Justice, Chancery Division, in the case of *Paul McCartney* vs. *John Lennon, George Harrison, Richard Starkey and Apple Corps Ltd.*

no defenses against Nems' retention of your royalties.

The present proposed settlement (which will cost you more than 1,500,000 pounds) was forced upon Klein, not induced by him.

These are the facts. I shall be more than pleased to give you chapter and verse, if you desire.

At least three of the Beatles didn't bother to reply to this letter.

CHAPTER SEVEN

Enter Pop Biz Demon Allen Klein

You get to Allen Klein's office by being whooshed to the forty-first floor of a high-rise building in the lox-and-bagels theater district of Broadway. When the elevator door opens, you step into a reception area which also serves as Klein's greenhouse, except that it is disguised by gross neo-Louis XIV mirrors and a film poster proclaiming the imminent arrival of the next superstar, Tony Anthony. A very forward little nymphet greets you with a nasal "Hi," delivered in her best Brooklyn dialect. Two or three idlers are lounging across her desk, whiling away the afternoon with a discussion about the color of George Harrison's socks. The nymphet reaches for her phone and asks for your names a second time, because with the distracting conversation about George's footwear, she's already forgotten them.

"Mista Schonfield and Mista McClay to see Mista Kloyn . . . sit down, he's still busy."

The girl is evidently bored with reception work. She catches the attention of a passing assistant.

"Will you tell Mista Kloyn that if he'd be koynd enough to send someone else out here, I'll place a little kiss on his big ass."

When the president of ABKCO (Allen and Betty Klein Co.) Industries is ready, his receptionist presses a buzzer under her desk. You are now permitted to pass through the security net, designed to stop an intruder from swiping any of Klein's early sixties gold records. This impressive array, including albums by Bobby Vinton, Herman's Hermits, Sam Cooke and the Rolling Stones, decorates the winding series of corridors leading to the pop biz king's ivory tower. Another Brooklyn receptionist, another buzz lock, and you are about to enter the lion's lair.

The door opens into a huge office overlooking the Hudson River from the George Washington Bridge to the Battery. A desk shaped like half a donut sits on the bright orange carpet. Behind it is a short, tubby figure in his late thirties, wearing checked trousers, a mock-turtleneck sweater and sneakers. He looks as if he's just come off the golf course. His face is boyish, despite an emerging double chin, and a little fifties forelock dangles across his brow. Nobody fits the description of "kinda cute" better than Allen Klein. He reminds George Harrison of Barney Rubble from the Flintstones, and Derek Taylor even describes him as cuddly.

"Fine view."

"Yup, you gotta have some compensation for this job," says Klein bluntly. His twinkling eyes grow momentarily brighter and he manages to pucker his lips into an inscrutable, yet almost cherubic, smile. The view is not his only compensation. He is deeply concerned with less aesthetic forms of reward. But Allen Klein loves to do business for its own sake. For him, going to work is the same thing as going to life. He's never happier than when he's doing a deal.

Although he keeps his desk immaculately clean and tidy, pens neatly arranged alongside his appointment book, he litters his office with a vast array of mementos. The toughest wheeler-dealer in the pop music business apparently likes to surround himself with tokens of his achievements and those of his clients. Beatle gold records are propped up on the window sill, a golden apple lies on his desk and the *Let It Be* Oscar is displayed on a shelf, alongside a row of books consisting entirely of best sellers, as if Klein suddenly decided that his office needed a little culture. It seems Klein is fortified by possessions, rather than pats on the back. He doesn't waste time socializing with the "faggy" elite of the pop world. When he leaves his office, his limousine usually zips straight back to his wife, three kids and an opulent Riverdale house, where the predominant color is violet. On the rare occasion that he gives a party, the guests are a strange ensemble of pop stars and Westchester dentists. Even at social functions, Klein never passes up an opportunity to talk business. He frequently works more than sixteen hours a day. When he reads over a paper, maybe some complex legal document, of which Klein has seen many, his little eyes dart back and forth across the page. He's oblivious to anything else. As he resumes the conversation, it's as if he's snapping out of a trance.

His secretary pokes her head around the door to remind him it's time for his lunch. The man who tends to put on weight doing business is out of his chair in an instant. He hitches his pants, pats his corpulent midriff and strides briskly across his forty-foot office into an empty paneled board room next door. He plonks himself down in an end seat, gulps his Coke and waits impatiently for his secretary to bring in his steak. When she enters with a tray, a little cloud darkens his day.

"What's this? Libby's tomato ketchup . . . we have Heinz, don't we?"

The secretary checks in a cupboard and returns with the required bottle. The little cloud passes.

Klein's meticulousness and facility for arithmetic are evident from the way he eats. On his plate are six chunks of steak, six onion rings and only five tomato slices. After a lightning computation of the plate's contents, Klein sets the meal in balance by chopping a tomato slice in half. Then, clutching his fork like a toothbrush, he spears a tomato slice, an onion ring and a piece of steak, dips the edibles into a glob of ketchup and devours a succulent mouthful. The final combination is on his fork ready to be demolished, when the telephone rings.

"Yep. Shit no. Tell him I said he's an asshole. Okay, I'll get to it right away," he blurts.

Klein gets up from his chair with surprising agility and strides back to his office. The items on his fork shiver like prisoners who have been pardoned at the last minute. Klein has forgotten all about them; business has commanded his attention completely.

Klein is a non-drinking hard worker, with an uncanny ability to sniff out pop business money, just as a bear can sniff out truffles. Although an accountant by profession, he claims to be even more skilled in legal matters. He is widely disliked and feared in the pop world, especially by those who have faced him across a bargaining table. He epitomizes Consciousness II, says one of his employees. A scrappy fighter with the instincts of a terrier, Klein bluffs, exaggerates, ducks most lawsuits with ease and comfortably goes the full fifteen rounds. Columbia Records' president, Clive Davis, whom Klein counts among his friends, once described him as an "alert, hard-working businessman, who has operated quite imaginatively in the record world." Others would say unscrupulously.

Klein's determination to succeed in business is almost fanatical, and a number of business opponents have felt the weight of the shrewd financial juggler's heel on their necks. Many of his enemies are concentrated on Wall Street, where he is regarded as a sharpie, according to a broker who has had dealings with him. Many people in his fortunate position would be tempted to take things easy. Not Allen Klein. The uncrowned king of the pop jungle is reputedly worth quite a few million dollars, but he has no intention of resting his bowling-pin physique in a haven in the sun. It's been a long, uphill struggle for the ABKCO president, but that's how he prefers it. He knows no other life.

Allen Klein was born in Newark on December 18, 1931. His mother died when he was two years old, and his father, a poor Jewish butcher, couldn't take care of his family and run the business at the same time. Klein and two of his three older sisters were placed in an orthodox Hebrew orphanage for ten years, until they went to live with their father again. (Thirty-eight years later, Klein told his assistant that if anybody at all was to attend the rehearsals for George Harrison's Madison Square Garden concert, it would be 20,000 orphans.) His nephew, Michael Kramer, says Klein's memories of those years in the orphanage are amazingly vivid and detailed. Even now, he still knows all the Hebrew services by heart, every single word, not just the *kiddush*.

Klein tends to live vicariously through young people. His manner of dress is one way in which he tries to recapture his lost youth. He continually refers back to details of his childhood, takes people to places he frequented as a boy, including even fast-food joints in New Jersey, and has a complete soda fountain in the den of his Riverdale house. As a child he ran into plenty of scrapes at school and was thrown out several times, according to Kramer. The parallels between his childhood and John Lennon's go far in explaining the rapport that the two have developed. Both were street-fighters, absented from their fathers. They came under a strong female influence other than their mothers'. In Klein's case, it was his mother's youngest sister, Helen. For Lennon, it was his Aunt Mimi.

After a brief spell in the army, Klein started work for a newspaper distributor in New Jersey. At the same time, he attended evening classes in accounting at Upsala College. He would fold his arms across his desk, put his head down and take a doze after a hard day's work. This used to irritate his Japanese professor. He would fire a question at his student, thinking that he was asleep. Klein would rattle back the correct answer without even lifting his head.

Klein joined the ranks of the many talented New York accountants, but he found himself a field, pop music, where they were in short supply. For a while he audited for a company handling Bobby Darin's account until he resigned to set up his own music publishing companies, handling the Shirelles' songs, among others. It wasn't long before he made the transition from bookkeeper to manager. His early artists included Sam Cooke and Bobby Vinton. Klein was soon reaping in the dollars and his reputation as a tough dealer grew with his bank account.

Although a tough business executive, he is considerably milder when dealing with family matters, his only other real interest. He has a characteristic, all-embracing Judaic concern for the welfare of his relatives. This only declines in intensity when he is preoccupied with his predominant interest—business. His young nephews adored him because he would bring home stacks of comic books for them every Friday and then take them to movies. They called him "Uncle Weasel."

But when Klein is obsessed with business, everything else is forgotten. His nephew Michael Kramer recalls that Klein took him to Philadelphia about eight years ago with popular AM disc jockey, Jocko (Doug Henderson). Kramer was abandoned all day in a motel room with nothing to do, while Uncle Allen took care of business. That evening, they went to a show with a top line-up for the times, Chubby Checker, the Orlons, Jimmy Soul and the Marvelettes. It lasted from six P.M. until two A.M. Klein spent the entire time negotiating in the theater office. At three A.M., young Kramer was awakened by a janitor, sweeping up in the balcony. He wandered around the dark theater until he found the office. Klein had forgotten all about him. On the way home, says Kramer, he insisted on stopping at a Toddle House, a place he used to go regularly when he was a youngster.

Kramer's mother, Esther, was the oldest of Klein's three sisters. She died of cancer three years ago. When Klein first visited her in the hospital, he found her room wasn't air-conditioned. He asked the director for an air-conditioned room for her, and was told there were none available. His offer to buy an air-conditioner for her room was rejected, as it was contrary to hospital policy. So was his generous and emotional gesture to buy air-conditioners for the entire hospital. In a moment of hyperbole, he offered to buy the hospital outright, before realizing the impracticability of such a step. Klein took his sister out of the hospital and found a doctor specializing in chemotherapy. He donated $10,000 to the doctor's research fund and his sister was kept alive for three more years. On the day she died, he took the kids out to play stickball, refusing to sit around and be miserable. The funeral took place a few days later in the pouring rain. As the mourners climbed into the limousine, the sun broke through the clouds.

"Oh my God, the sun's out!" Klein exclaimed suddenly and to the amazement of his relatives broke down.

"You had to see a man like this cry," one relative said.

Klein was bitterly upset when his favored nephew, Ronnie Schneider, who had been comfortably reaping the reward of his uncle's efforts, left ABKCO with Klein's prized clients, the Rolling Stones. Schneider's term with the Stones was brief, and afterward he found he was no longer welcome at the Broadway office. Michael Kramer became the prime focus of Klein's nepotism, but his working hours were doubled. He says he once made the mistake of taking a vacation in London with his uncle. Klein kept him working every available hour each day, until the last day of the trip. In desperation, he sneaked away from the office, jumped into a cab and told the driver: "Show me the town."

"Allen just never stops," he says. "I've turned down offers of vacations with him ever since. A few months ago, we were seated at different tables at a *bar mitzvah*. Allen became restless. He sneaked across to my table and spent four hours with me solving the McCartney problem for the fiftieth time."

Klein's driving ambition and energy have steered him successfully through many perilous twists and turns in the business world. Whenever he does business, the air is likely to be darkened by writs. Although he has been served with over forty lawsuits, only a few have stuck. Most just bounce off. His tumultuous business history, documented in the Bishop's report commissioned by Leonard Richenberg, found its way to the pages of the London

127

Sunday Times. It didn't help his image in the austere financial circles of London.

"I was broke when I was hit with all these writs," says Klein offhandedly. "They made a meal outta nothin'."

Unfortunately for Allen Klein, a New York federal district court found him guilty on ten counts of failing to file employees' withholding taxes just as Paul McCartney's suit for a dissolution of the Beatles' partnership was being heard by an English court. The British newspapers lost no time printing the story. Klein emphasizes that he had paid the tax. He was prosecuted for failure to file a return, a duty which he claims was delegated to a member of his staff. He is appealing the conviction.

Even before he handled the Beatles' business affairs, Allen Klein had achieved renown in the United States through his involvement with a small Philadelphia recording firm with a poor earnings record—the Cameo-Parkway Record Company. The story of Cameo and Klein is still heard on Wall Street, especially when brokers' conversations swing to the subject of surprisingly rapid stock price climbs. Klein bought a chunk of Cameo-Parkway when he was president of Allen Klein and Company, a New York-based entertainment outfit, whose main source of revenue resulted from the sale of distribution rights of discs to major recording companies. Its principal assets were the recording rights to the Rolling Stones and Herman's Hermits in addition to 150,000 Metro-Goldwyn-Mayer shares, worth several million dollars. Klein was also a fairly enterprising music publisher, though a less successful film producer. His prosperity was attributed to good personal relations with artists and producers, particularly with the Rolling Stones. Such an equitable situation was not destined to last. The Stones eventually broke with Klein and hit him with a lawsuit which is still pending.

The Cameo-Parkway story kept many a *Wall Street Journal* reporter busy. On July 28, 1967, Klein purchased 297,000 shares, or 48 percent of Cameo-Parkway, at $1.75 a share. His cohort, Abbey Butler, a young rising star in a Wall Street brokerage house, acquired another 50,000 shares, or 8.1 percent. During the next few months, Cameo announced proposed acquisitions of Al-

len Klein and Company, Merco Enterprises Incorporated
and, most important, Chappell Enterprises, the huge music
publishing concern, which was up for grabs. The price of
Cameo shares climbed rapidly from 3⅞ to a high of 53
in the third quarter of 1967. In the final quarter, it fluc-
tuated from 29½ to 64⅝. In the first few weeks of 1968,
it zoomed to an all-time high of 76⅝, before the Securities and Exchange Commission suspended trading in
Cameo shares on February 23, when the price was
55⅛. The volume of shares traded during the above period was 2,047,900, although during this time there were
only a maximum of 240,000 shares available for public
trading. The commission's decision was deemed necessary
in the public interest "in the absence of adequate information necessary for shareholders and prospective investors
to make an informed investment judgment."

Cameo didn't take over either Merco or Chappell. It
became apparent that the company didn't have the resources for so momentous an achievement as taking over
the world's largest music publishing firm. But Cameo did
make one acquisition—Allen Klein and Company—in a
reverse takeover in September 1968. Klein rechristened
the single resulting company ABKCO Industries Incorporated. The American Stock Exchange declines to list its
shares on the grounds that its earnings and net worth do
not meet the required standards. The shares are currently
traded over-the-counter.

A special meeting of shareholders was held to consider
the merger of Cameo and Klein and Company. The proxy
statement for the meeting made the following charitable
comment:

In October, 1967, the management of Cameo announced that an agreement in principle had been
reached whereby Klein and Company would be com-
bined with Cameo. Before consideration of this transaction proceeded beyond a very preliminary stage,
Mr. Klein and the management of Cameo became
involved in discussions looking to the possible acquisition of certain unrelated corporations. . . . It is
possible that the articles appearing in the press,

including those concerning the combination of Cameo and Klein and Company, may have influenced the price of Cameo common stock during the period prior to February 23, 1968.

Not everybody was satisfied with that explanation. One company, Lucarelli Enterprises, and one of its principal shareholders, had already filed a five million dollar lawsuit against Klein, Butler, a former stockholder of Cameo, and others. The defendants were charged with conspiring to interest Lucarelli in the acquisition of the controlling capital stock interest in Cameo, for the purpose of stimulating public interest in the company and its publicly held shares, in order to cause an artificial rise in their price. On November 1, 1967, the suit against Klein, Butler and Cameo was dismissed for failure by the plaintiffs to state a claim upon which relief could be granted.

Allen Klein sums up the whole Cameo-Parkway story in one sentence.

"You can be wrong and you don't have to say you're sorry," he says with a chuckle.

Kramer says Klein originally planned to sell Allen Klein and Company to MGM, become president of that ample corporation, then sell MGM to Xerox and ultimately sit on the board of Xerox. But Klein found the pop business more suited to his uncompromising style. He stumbled across the Rolling Stones in the spring of 1965, when the Stones' managers, Eric Easton and Andrew Oldham, sought his services in renegotiating the Stones' recording contract with Decca. The Decca executives paled before the truculent little whizz-kid and agreed to part with $1,250,000 in advance royalties. A dispute blew up over the disposition of the money. Oldham claimed that Nanker Phelge Music Ltd., a company owned by himself and the Rolling Stones, was entitled to receive the $1,250,000. But the sum had been paid to another Nanker Phelge Music Ltd., an American subsidiary of Allen Klein and Company, under an agreement which Klein claimed related to the distribution of the Rolling Stones' records. Klein eventually settled with Oldham, but the Stones continue to unleash writs.

At one time, the Stones were very contented to have Allen Klein holding their contracts, but eventually they joined the ever-growing contingent of musicians, now including Paul McCartney and James Taylor, who have no love for him. Many rock stars, however, have found Allen Klein's money-making services irresistible. Klein functions as a middleman, exercising his brashness and bargaining skills with the royalty-rich record companies in return for a fat percentage. He claims to get much better deals for the musicians he takes under his umbrella. He also seems to be very influential in persuading the dope-conscious American customs officials that his artists with drug convictions are not such bad guys that they should be banned from the United States.

Always at Klein's right hand, aiding in the various business tangles, is his lawyer and ABKCO vice-president, Harold Seider. One ABKCO employee says Seider "tones down Klein a lot," especially when the top man tends to go on a bit, expounding the many strategies which occupy his nimble brain. Shortly before George Harrison's Madison Square Garden concert, Klein was sitting by his swimming pool, rambling on about his plans for the event. Seider sat quietly reading a newspaper, paying no attention and simply saying "Yes, Allen" about once every thirty seconds. Finally, Seider put down his paper, did a mock calculation of the concert gate and said: "Just think, Allen, eight billion rupees. It's the biggest thing ever." Klein's reaction was to drench Seider with his root beer.

Apart from Seider, Klein's other close friend is John Lennon. He places no expense restraints on John and Yoko when they come to New York. One ABKCO employee finds them both a very big headache. When they want malteds, for example, he says, they order ten dollars' worth.

The employee throws his arms wide apart to emphasize that he considers John Lennon a "gigantic hypocrite."

"That line in his song 'Imagine no possessions,' that's such bullshit," says the disillusioned assistant. "When John comes to New York, he tries to buy Manhattan. And as for 'Working Class Hero,' that line about 'keep you doped with religion and sex and TV,' my God, he watches TV twenty-three hours a day."

Allen Klein, however, has great respect and admiration for Lennon, and describes him as "the real article." He has even written a few lines to one of Lennon's songs, "How Do You Sleep," a biting attack on Paul McCartney.

"I told John he was losing his credibility with things such as 'Power to the People, Right On,'" says Klein proudly.

Lennon was initially attracted to Klein because of the similarity of their backgrounds. At first, he said he trusted Klein as much as he trusted any businessman. Now it is apparent that he not only trusts Klein, but likes him and is amused by him. Such affection from John Lennon has been achieved by few businessmen.

"He's highly sensitive as well as highly intelligent," says John. "Anything other than the music business, he has a complete block on. This irritates me sometimes when I try and sing him a song and he can't hear it until it's a finished record. But he's a creative artist in the way that he will put people together, like me and Phil Spector.

"I believe him when he says he has helped Sam Cooke's old father.* I think he's a sentimental old Jewish mommy. He tries hard to understand Yoko and her work, but it's just a struggle for him. It's taken him a long time to come 'round and realize she just isn't another chick. Now, if anything, he's realized she's at least his equal."

Yoko says Klein once told her that if he wound up managing the Beatles, he wouldn't mind John having a little fun on the side with her.

"I was almost flattered," she declared. "I thought, 'Oh, my God, I must look young.'"

"Allen never talks down to people," John continued. "He doesn't play that game which Richenberg and Eastman both play, that 'We're here to help you.' He likes to have a laugh with the lads. You can't imagine Richenberg doin' anything but playin' golf or crushin' beetles. Allen's human, whereas the others, they're not human, they're

---

* Sam Cooke was being managed by Klein when the singer was shot in a motel.

automatons. You can tickle Allen, and I couldn't imagine
tickling Richenberg or Eastman."

Whatever Lennon feels about Klein now, his main reason for hiring him in 1969 was that he didn't wish to go
through bankruptcy proceedings like Mickey Rooney. John
was much impressed with the cleanup that Klein instituted
at Apple. Much less impressed, however, was Nat Weiss.

"I had lunch with Klein and his cronies just prior to his
takeover of Apple," says Weiss. "I knew Klein was going
to succeed. He had to. His timing was so good. At Apple
he was like Mussolini, making the trains run on time.
Klein is a creature of instinct, who likes to intimidate you,
just to see how far he can go. George keeps telling me
how great Klein is, because he's made him all this money.
I just told him not to bother trying to sell Klein to me."

Klein brought a new uncertainty to Apple and the
possibility of eagle-sudden dismissals. Apple employees
gaped in disbelief as they saw their idyllic employment
situations crumble. Chris O'Dell was an Apple secretary
when Klein brought his Seventh Avenue urgency to the
damasked drawing rooms of the Mayfair townhouse. She
observed that he wasn't prone to bouts of nostalgia.

"He just moved in and started firing people," she said.
"It took him more than a year to do it, but in that time
he got rid of everybody he could possibly clear out,
either by taking their work away, so that there was
nothing for them to do, or by making their jobs so un-
comfortable they felt obliged to quit. He didn't like people
who were close to the Beatles. He was worried they would
go back and report to them. As soon as Ron Kass [head
of Apple Records] went, everybody was worried. [Klein
later said he was nice to Kass for letting him leave.]
Klein was really mean. He fired people when they were
on vacation. The only survivors were Neil Aspinall and
Mal Evans. They'd been with the Beatles from the beginning."

When Klein first arrived, he apparently found it hard
to believe that Aspinall was not an aspiring status-seeker
threatening his authority. It took some time before he
realized that here was an old friend of the Beatles, who
wouldn't play power games. Chris O'Dell believes George

Harrison wasn't too thrilled with Klein at first meeting either, but he went along with John.

"One night, I was at George's house shortly after Klein arrived," she says. "Klein came over to talk for a while. After he left I told George I didn't like him. He said, 'Yeah, you know he's a businessman, but he's making us money.'

"As time went by the atmosphere at Apple became terrible," she continued. "Nobody ever really saw Klein. The first time I found out what he looked like was when I saw his picture in the papers."

Klein knew how to appeal to the Beatles, or at least three of them. When Lee Eastman lost his temper with Klein, the little New York accountant just sat quietly looking sheepish, while his character was torn to shreds. Three of the Beatles jumped to his side. As Derek Taylor said: "They were always prepared to side with the underdog."

But Klein cut a less sympathetic figure with Paul McCartney. He was also widely hated by all levels of Apple employees, who were being fired at random, unless they could prove themselves either indispensable or harmless. Some of Klein's dismissals were later regretted. Tea girls were dismissed and then it was discovered there was no tea. Klein defended his actions with the simple explanation that when you've got to reorganize, somebody's going to get hurt. He claimed the Beatles wanted to be rid of the leeches, but were embarrassed to fire them, so they asked him to do it. After a ten-month reign, he proclaimed the company had never been in better shape. By this time, most of the freeloaders were out. "Magic Alex" was no longer the "original mad inventor" at Apple electronics. The ebb of funds through the company's front door had been stopped. Apple had lost nearly one million dollars in its first year, whereas in ten months, Klein declared, he had made the Beatles ten million.

Some of Klein's boasts may have been justified, others deserve further scrutiny. Although he had settled the Nems dispute and freed the Beatles from the merchant bankers, his claim that he had made them ten million dollars was based on the outcome of the Northern Songs bid battle.

The ten million was simply the amount the Beatles received from the sale of their shares in that company. Not long after the Beatles sold their Northern Songs' shares to ATV, Klein lambasted Brian Epstein as a bad businessman, who took too long to negotiate record contracts. It was Epstein, however, who had ensured that the Beatles held shares in Northern Songs to begin with. In view of this, Klein's statement about the Beatles' first manager makes little or no sense, since at the time those shares were sold, they accounted for a large part of John and Paul's assets. In effect, Klein was saying that the man who secured them this valuable investment was a fool.

"Epstein only made the Beatles seven million pounds in all that time," Klein wailed, throwing his arms up to the heavens as if to demand celestial confirmation of that statement. "Since I took over I made them nine million in just a little time. The Beatles had outgrown Epstein, like they outgrew that other fella, the arranger. What was his name? Martin. What's George Martin done since, I ask yer? The Beatles wanted to pack up with Epstein because their contract was up, but Epstein planned to ensure they couldn't do it."

Klein wasn't prepared to elaborate on that statement. He dried up very suddenly, adding only that he hoped the results would speak for themselves. It is only fair to add that the Beatles have never made any such comment about their first manager. Klein never gave Epstein any credit for creating a valuable world-wide music phenomenon, which he was fortunate enough to inherit three parts of. While Epstein was transforming four scruffy boys from a Liverpool cellar club into the greatest show business act of the sixties, and displaying an incredible amount of foresight about the future of popular music, Klein was locked in a tacky back-office of a Philadelphia theater, negotiating a small-time deal. For a man as skilled at business and knowledgeable about the music scene as Allen Klein, such blindness to Epstein's talent is surprising, unless, of course, he feels obliged to play down Epstein's achievements in order to enhance his own.

Klein's explanation for wanting to manage the Beatles

in the first place is very simple. "Anybody in this business would want to manage them. Don't you want the best?" he adds wryly. "I went straight to Lennon when he said they were goin' broke. Yup, outta the clear blue. John Eastman was already there and the old man [Lee Eastman] arrived soon after. You can be sure they wanted to take over as managers.

"I baited Lee Eastman a bit," says Klein gleefully. "He blew his cool, started screamin' and cursin' at me. That settled it. They knew what he was like then, all except Paul."

Klein's feud with the Eastman family was far too unsophisticated for the likes of "Our Crowd." It was more like the savage battles between the Ozark families, the McCoys and the Hatfields. Eastman would invite Klein to meetings at such elitist establishments as the Harvard Club and the University Club, places in which Allen Klein would scarcely feel at ease. Klein favored more direct techniques, such as noncooperation and blatant disregard for the Eastmans' suggestions. For a while John Eastman and Klein maintained some semblance of civility toward each other, although Lee Eastman blasted Klein at their first meeting. By September 1969, every slight vestige of basic business courtesy had been swept away. One of Klein's letters to John Eastman at this time read:*

Dear John: I am on a diet, so please stop putting words in my mouth. Your misuse and abuse of the truth is almost without parallel. . . .

Lee Eastman resorted to the lowest forms of animal life in order to describe Klein.

"I won't do business with him, he's a swine," Eastman declared. "When you go to bed with a louse, you get lousy."

"We cooperated with Klein for about two weeks," says his son, John. "Do you know what he did? It was agreed

---

* Letter submitted before the English High Court of Justice, Chancery Division, in the case of *Paul McCartney* vs. *John Lennon, George Harrison, Richard Starkey and Apple Corps Ltd.*

that both of us [Eastman and Klein] would see all the Beatles' documents, but Klein took out all the important stuff and sent along a huge bundle of documents containing nothing of importance. Klein is impossible to deal with. I'm convinced that when he opens his mouth, he doesn't know what's going to come out."

"He's right, I don't," said Klein, rather ruefully, while Lennon exploded in hysterics. "Yup, I ripped off those documents, damn right! But Eastman and McCartney had already gone behind our backs buying Northern Songs shares.

"Lee Eastman has achieved a lot," Klein concedes. "I give credit where it's due. But you play to win, right? And if you lose, well, you don't try to kill everybody. That's what Eastman did. His attitude was, 'If I can't get anything, I'm going to make it as difficult as possible for everybody else.' Pure harassment!

"Paul was too easily led by the Eastmans [Lee and John]. But he's not anymore. Now Paul's too easily led by Linda. She's leading him down the road. She even calls the sidemen for his album. 'We'd like to audition you,' she says. Paul is about two years behind John right now. John was just as heavily influenced by Yoko at one time, but that's not so anymore. I pried John away from Yoko, artistically. There'll be no more John and Yoko twin albums.

"McCartney is an ideas' man. You can't underestimate his talent, but it was Lennon who completed many of his ideas. The trouble with Paul's albums is that his ego won't allow him to use anyone good to bounce ideas off. George used Phil Spector and Eric Clapton. With Ringo's single, I told George, 'You've got to work with him, he needs help.'

"I've done a lot for Ringo," says Klein, getting into his stride and taking steadily larger gulps on his Coca-Cola. "Do you know anyone who would have offered him a leading film part? I did. I didn't even send him the script. I said, 'Meet the director and if that's okay, let me know.' He went to Europe, met the guy and they got on really well. After half an hour, he said, 'It's good, let's call Allen.'"

Klein suddenly feels obliged to apologize for his lack of modesty.

"I used to play down my deals," he says. "I took a lot of shit from the English papers. The London *Sunday Times* really did a hatchet job on me. Later they wrote another piece about the way I was running Apple. It was almost an apology. Now I've decided to say what I think. John wanted to do his *Rolling Stone* interview for me, because I hadn't spoken up."

A conversation with the ABKCO president can prove a mind-boggling experience. He proves each point by pulling thick files out of his drawer and shuffling through mounds of paper. Occasionally, he pulls an old envelope from his back pocket and does a rapid calculation to show how his brilliant deals worked out in his favor. He's impossible to pin down.

"Don't talk to me about management," he says. "Talk to me about net and gross." His voice takes on a distinctly metallic edge, and that cherubic smile dances across his lips as he sees he's made his point.

"I made the boys lots of money," he boasts, reverting to his favorite topic of conversation. *"Let It Be* made more money for them than all the other films put together. They wanted it for TV, but I told 'em that was stoopid.

"Before they met me, they were being fucked around by everybody. I did a great deal with Capitol and E.M.I. They knew they couldn't stop an artist recording. So up went the royalty rates. We account for over fifty percent of Capitol Records' business. They're just our distributors. I did Capitol a great favor. I delivered them product. These boys want to work, but you have to motivate them. They won't work while they're bein' screwed by a record company. But when somebody gets rid of the bullshit, and they're getting a fair deal, they'll work."

Klein's renegotiating of the Beatles' recording contract was unquestionably a big money-winner for them. He claims that even McCartney congratulated him on the deal. The industrious accountant is doubtless top-man at bargaining with, or bullying, record companies. But he is a business manager, rather than an artist's manager.

"He made them lots of money, sure," says one observer.

"But he alienated McCartney and the Beatles broke up. Paul is a difficult bastard to deal with, but somehow Brian Epstein handled him."

Klein still hasn't given up hope with McCartney.

"The Beatles could get together, but only if Paul matures and stops looking for all this middle-class bullshit," he says.

No chance, say most other observers.

Klein might also have a problem getting John Lennon together with Paul.

"It's a house we own together and there's no way of settling it, unless we all decide to live in it," says Lennon. "We only ever wrote together 'cause in the early days it was fun and later on convenient. But our best songs were always written alone. We'd been workin' apart ever since we'd been workin' together. It'll never happen, there's no use contemplating it. If I'm friends with him again, I'll never write with him again. There's no point. I might write with Yoko because she's in the same room as me. I was livin' with Paul, so I wrote with him. He writes with Linda, he's livin' with her. It's just natural. In five years, hell, you wake up."

Klein still nurtures the hope that McCartney will come around. In the meantime, his defeat in the English courts gnaws at him.

"My friend, Johnny Eastman, won the first round," he says bitingly. "But it was a victory in PR. The trouble was the establishment was against us. The establishment, the fuckin' courts, the government, they can all exercise what's known as discretion, when they don't wanna face the facts.

"I knew the partnership would be dissolved. I know the English law. The only reason for opposing it was the horrendous tax consequences that could result. But that old judge, Stamp [Justice Stamp appointed the receiver], he didn't understand what it was all about. He got lost. He got Beatlemania."

Klein is once again rummaging through papers when George Harrison bursts into his office, just arrived from London and wearing an outrageous pair of Italian sunglasses. Klein drops everything he's doing, leaps up from his chair and gives George a big greeting. Immediately, he tries to interest him in business matters. George, however, is already immersed in conversation with Lennon, who is bubbling like a teen-ager over his new boots. The president of ABKCO Industries waves his arms in despair. Yoko is still screaming down the phone.

Eventually, George is ready to talk business, but not before he's voiced a concern of his own. He has a complaint about the various groupies sitting outside the building that houses the ABKCO office.

"Allen, can't you get rid of those ABKCO scruffs?" he asks politely. "They're bad for our image. They don't have the class of Apple scruffs."

Allen Klein is stumped for words, a very rare occurrence.

CHAPTER EIGHT

"It's Only a Northern Song"

"I'm not going to be fucked around by men in suits sitting on their fat arses in the City."

John Lennon's angry challenge to the world of big business in the spring of 1969 summed up the Beatles' bitterness when they started playing "Monopoly for real money." Their frustrated attempt to gain control of Northern Songs helped tear them apart, and alienated them once and for all from the business establishment they mistrusted and grew to despise.

For years each had drawn 100 pounds weekly pocket money "in green" and left it at that. But now, all of a sudden they wanted more. They wanted control of a twenty-four-million-dollar public company. Northern Songs was part of them. It was them. They felt almost entitled to it.

Northern Songs had been created by Brian Epstein and music publisher Dick James in January 1963. It went public on the London Stock Exchange in 1965. The main idea behind the flotation was to provide the Beatles some sort of "paper" security. Brian Epstein may not have been a sophisticated financier, but he appreciated the advantages of turning highly taxed income into capital gain.

After the flotation John and Paul each retained fifteen percent of the company's five million shares, a bundle worth 267,000 pounds [$640,000] apiece at the time of issue. George Harrison and Ringo Starr held 1.6 percent between them—worth some 27,000 pounds. Nems retained 7.5 percent. Northern Songs' chairman was accountant Charles Silver and Dick James was managing director. Together, they controlled 37½ percent of Northern, valued at $1,687,500 at the time of issue.

Dick James had given up pursuing stardom as a singer. Having gone bald, he found even his toupee was wearing a bit thin with the fans in the front row. He was struggling in the Tin Pan Alley when Brian Epstein walked into his office in 1962 with a demonstration disc of "Please, Please Me." The Beatles had been offered to just about every major publisher and been turned down. But James could not afford to turn away business. As he put it: "I flipped." He never looked back.

From the start the Beatles' creative energy put dynamism into Northern's profit growth. In four years they added more than one hundred songs to the company's original catalogue of fifty-nine compositions, even though their contract only demanded a minimum of six songs a year. John and Paul claimed half their writers' share of the copyright profits via a company called Maclen Music Ltd., forty percent owned by each of them and twenty percent held by Apple. Originally, the two Beatles owned a company called Lenmac Enterprises, which had the rights on the first fifty-nine songs they composed. But Lenmac was acquired by Northern before its flotation, and recent attempts by Paul McCartney to buy it back have so far failed.

The Beatles' attempts to buy Northern Songs began when Allen Klein—"I'm not the new Epstein, I'm the old Allen"—moved into Apple to sort out the mess. But as soon as Klein appeared on the scene, Beatles' assets seemed, as he said, to walk. First Nems was acquired by Triumph. Then, Charles Silver and Dick James sold out to Associated Television Corporation, which went on to bid nine million pounds for the rest of Northern.

Sir Lew Grade, the well-known showman and impresario, had created ATV. He was king of a multi-million-dollar communications and entertainments empire, but he had no music to crown his glory. He had lost a long takeover battle for Chappell, the music publishers, to Phillips, the electronics giant. So if he couldn't have Gershwin, he would get the Beatles. Sir Lew had approached Dick James with an offer for his shares several months before. The two men knew each other well. Grade had handled James in the fifties when he was a show business agent and James a singer. After the disappointment of losing Chappell, Sir Lew thought of James. But James was not interested. He promised, however, that if he ever did want to sell or "do some kind of partnership deal" he would go to Sir Lew.

He was a worried man when he finally went to Sir Lew in March 1969. John Eastman says he was scared that Klein might try and get control of Northern. There had been some nasty exchanges—even talk of litigation between the Beatles and James. Attempts to get the Beatles to extend their contracts with the company had failed and relations with them were strained, to say the least. So James sought refuge with ATV.

"Although he was scared of Klein, James had made his fortune on those two kids [John and Paul]," says John Eastman. "I told him he was a bastard to sell to Grade."

The Beatles agreed. They had no idea that James was planning to sell. That he had done so without first consulting them made them furious. And as for Associated Television Corporation, a household name in communications and entertainment, they saw it as an unforgiveable sellout to the establishment. John Lennon first learned the shattering news from the papers on March 28. While Paul

143

was honeymooning with Linda somewhere in the States and could not be reached, John was on public display, in bed with Yoko, staging a demonstration for peace. At just a mention of Sir Lew Grade's name, John forgot all about acorns and his peace message. ATV's bid brought out the fighter in him. "I won't sell," he declared. "They are my shares and my songs and I want to keep a bit of the end product. I don't have to ring Paul. I know damn well he feels the same as I do."

Jack Gill, ATV's astute and soft-spoken finance director, had started negotiations with James and Silver one morning in mid-March. After the meeting, Jack Gill rang through to Sir Lew. "The deal's dead," he said. "There are too many complications." Sir Lew went in personally that afternoon. "I got there ten minutes early with Jack," he said. "Dick James and Charles Silver arrived before our lawyers and theirs and our representatives from the bank. Very simply I said, 'Don't let's mess about, let's do the deal now,' and I made them a proposition. It took exactly five minutes and they said, 'You got a deal.' Then our lawyers came in, and our bankers and brokers. It was a waste of time because we'd done the deal. That's exactly how long it took—five minutes."

John and Paul rang Allen Klein, who was enjoying a brief break in Puerto Rico. What should they do? How were they going to stop ATV and get Northern for themselves? Klein rushed back to London. So did John, Paul and Yoko. Together, they went to see the London merchant bankers, Henry Ansbacher and Company, and were introduced to a Mr. Bruce Ormrod, their luckless adviser in the incredible bid battle that followed. Mr. Ormrod, or "Sergeant Ormrod" as he was later nicknamed, is a tall, lean, somewhat excitable individual. He clearly found dealing with the Beatles and their "manager," Allen Klein, trying and confusing at best, highly embarrassing and awkward most of the time. Unaided except for a junior assistant who tagged along at the meetings, Mr. Ormrod tried his best to find "a City solution" to the Beatles' problem. He excelled himself during one crucial period in the Northern Songs saga by almost clinching a sensible deal between the Beatles and a group of London institutions which owned a block of Northern Songs that could have given the Beatles control. He almost did it, but not quite. The agreement was on paper and awaiting the autographs of John, Paul, George and Ringo. Then John delivered his epitaph on the City: "I'm not going to be fucked around by men in suits sitting on their fat arses in the City," and the deal fell through.

For openers, ATV and the Beatles were fairly evenly matched in their Northern shareholdings. ATV had bought 1,604,750 shares from Silver and James, and with its own 137,000 holding, claimed nearly 35 percent of the company. The Beatles controlled 29.7 percent and could muster another 0.6 percent from Beatle company holdings. Paul McCartney had 751,000 shares; John Lennon owned 644,000 and held another 50,000 as trustee; Ringo Starr had 40,000. George Harrison sold his in March 1968 when his song-writing contract with Northern expired, but his wife Patricia held 1,000. Subafilms, a company controlled by Apple Corps, had 30,000. Triumph Investment Trust found itself the happy owner of a strategic block of 237,000 shares—4.7 percent of the company—inherited from its acquisition of Nems in February that year.

The Beatles were not in a position to make an all-out counter bid. It would have cost them at least 9.5 million pounds in hard cash, and that kind of money they simply did not have. Besides, to acquire the whole company would have defeated their purpose of controlling a nice secure publicly quoted vehicle for Apple Corps. Yet by April tenth it was obvious—judging by their protracted talks with "Sergeant Ormrod" and "Captain Klein" at Ansbacher's—that a counter bid was what they had in mind. Mr. Ormrod was quoted as saying he thought they had "a sporting chance of success," while Sir Lew Grade, characteristically unruffled by this dramatic turn of events, pointed out that ATV had thirty-five percent of Northern and would not let go of that "for anything."

The Beatles pressed on, determined to play the game —"Monopoly for real money" John Lennon called it—by the broker's rules. But neither Sir Lew nor the Beatles knew at the time that a third force had muscled into their power struggle for Northern. As soon as ATV had laid its bid cards on the table, the professionals—brokers and investment fund managers acting for their clients—pulled up their chairs for a game of poker. Northern's share price soared as institutions went to the stock market, politely elbowing one another to pick up a few shares on speculation or to increase their holdings in anticipation of a cash bid from the Beatles or a forced increase in ATV's offer. Market dealers in the shares soon identified the buyers and put them in touch with each other. A powerful syndicate of institutional shareholders in Northern was formed and met in secret to discuss what to do as each "happening" took place. It did not reveal its hand—fourteen percent of Northern's shares—until weeks later when it drove a wedge between ATV and the Beatles, forcing a stalemate which went on for months.

The Syndicate, or Consortium, comprised clients of three leading London brokerage firms, Astaire and Company, W. I. Carr, and Spencer Thornton. The clients of these brokers had widely differing interests and these imposed strains on the Consortium's position later in the game. Astaire's clients, theater owners Howard and Wyndham, played perhaps the most active, and in the end, decisive, role in the affair. Howard and Wyndham had bought up some five percent of Northern in the market during February and March, a beautifully timed initiative taken by American show business lawyer, Ralph Fields. A fair number of the Northern shares picked up by Howard and Wyndham must have drifted onto the market from Clive Epstein's holdings, which had been skimmed off Nems' original 7.5 percent stake in Northern when Triumph bought Nems in February.

Fields saw the potential in a song catalogue of Beatle hits, including such evergreens as "Michelle" and "Yesterday." The other institutional members of the Consortium, including Ebor Unit Trust, the Slater Walker Invan Trust, and merchant bankers Arbuthnot Latham, were skeptical at first. Many had been sitting on the bulk of their shares since the time of the flotation four years earlier, and would have been happy to let ATV have them for a few shillings more. But Fields argued that such songs, like good wine, would appreciate with age and that the institutions would

146

do well to retain their holdings while securing new "independent" management for Northern to humor the Beatles—who, after all, had a big say, given that they were the company's main assets. Eventually, Fields managed to persuade the other members of this newly formed Beatle Fan Club to hold out for more cash for their shares from ATV, or better still, to try to do a deal with the Beatles.

The Consortium had one link with the Beatles—or at least with Paul McCartney. Lee Eastman, as it happened, was known to Astaire's. But that did not help, and even hindered their chances of communicating with the others, especially with John Lennon and Allen Klein, who dictated policy to all except McCartney in the Beatle camp. Edgar Astaire, a senior partner of his firm, a man with a wry sense of the ridiculous, recalls one occasion when he took Lee Eastman to lunch at Les Ambassadeurs in London's West End, only to be confronted by John, Yoko and Allen Klein, who trouped into the restaurant in between dessert and coffee.

"It was all very jovial," recalls Astaire. "I must admit I didn't really understand very much of what was going on. I remember offering John a cigarette and he seemed to object to the fact that I didn't roll my own. He also said that we could not talk sensibly because I wore a suit." Bafflement all 'round. There all direct communication between the City men and the Beatles ended. Mr. Astaire did, however, meet Paul McCartney on another occasion and thought him "a very reasonable chap."

The events leading up to the Beatles' offer took place in quick succession from April tenth to April twenty-fourth, when they called a price of 212½ pence cash per Northern share. On April tenth they issued a statement: Individually and collectively they opposed ATV's bid and were "consulting their financial advisors with a view to making a counter offer." They had thirty percent of Northern, which, they pointed out menacingly, was "heavily dependent for its revenue" on the royalties from Beatle song compositions. They "strongly advised" shareholders to sit tight and wait for their offer.

Next day, S. G. Warburg, merchant bank acting for

147

ATV, sent out a formal fifteen-page document to share-holders. ATV's share price rose 10 pence in the market, making the value of ATV's loan stock and cash offer some 196 pence per Northern share. The offer would remain open until May second.

On April twelfth, John and Yoko dropped in at Ansbacher's office, a stone's throw away from Warburg's. Both were dressed in white, wearing sneakers, their hair falling about their shoulders. Freaks come to the City. Purpose of the meeting: to establish a basis for the Beatles' bid and to work out rather complicated financing arrangements to pay for it. April fifteenth saw more talks at Ansbacher's, again attended by John and Yoko, driven in a distinctive white Rolls-Royce with a television aerial. With them was the stocky figure of Allen Klein, dressed in a polo-neck sweater. Next day, Northern's share price soared on the theory that a third party, other than the Beatles and ATV, was interested in bidding for the company. News got around the market that certain institutions were shopping for Northern Songs.

Friday, April eighteenth: The Beatles announced that they would bid for control only. This news caught specula-tors by surprise and Northern's share price dropped. De-tails of the Beatles' offer were not released despite day-long talks, which continued over the weekend. Suggestions that there had been angry meetings at Ansbacher's, with Paul storming off in a huff, were denied. Ormrod said the dis-cussions were neither disorganized nor quarrelsome, but added ruefully, "It is always more difficult to deal with individuals."

But the rumblings at Ansbacher's were true. Paul was being advised by the Eastmans to sit tight. "There was no point in putting out cash to get control of the com-pany," said John Eastman. "Those song copyrights were invaluable."

April nineteenth: Details of the Beatles' offer trickled through to the press. The bid was being mounted on their behalf by three Beatle companies, Apple Corps, equally owned by the four, Subafilms, 76.1 percent owned by Apple, and Maclen (Music), 20 percent owned by Apple with Paul McCartney and John Lennon controlling the balance in equal proportions.

On April twentieth, a monumental row took place at Ansbacher's. Paul McCartney refused to commit his shares in Northern Songs as part of the necessary collateral for the loan advanced by Ansbacher's to finance the Beatles' bid. Ormrod and Klein agreed that the solidarity of the Beatles in making their offer must be stressed all down the line. McCartney's action had to be interpreted as nothing more than caution. Klein later said Lee Eastman had persuaded Paul not to put up his shares.

April twenty-fourth: The Beatles announced the broad lines of their offer. The non-monetary incentives were that they would extend their contracts with Northern for a further two years and would weld rich Beatle assets into it if they got control. They snubbed ATV's offer and stated that they would "not be happy to continue, let alone renew, their existing contracts with Northern under the aegis of ATV." Their feelings were being understated, to put it mildly.

While ATV's bid was too low and therefore "unacceptable" to the Consortium, the Beatles' offer was a non-starter for other, more complex reasons. For one thing they were going for a maximum of one million shares only, or twenty percent more of the company, enough to secure control. Here was a principal weakness and ATV hammered relentlessly at it during the ensuing battle.

The point was that ATV, with thirty-five percent of Northern in its pocket, had the power to make or break the Beatles' offer. If everyone but ATV had accepted it, it might have been an attractive deal. Shareholders would have got 212½ pence cash for every four out of seven shares turned in. The remaining shares held in public hands would have found a scarcity value on the market, with ATV locked in with thirty-five percent and the Beatles with fifty-one percent. But if ATV, too, decided to throw its holdings to the Beatles, the proportion of shares that the Beatles could have taken of any one person's holdings would have gone down to two out of seven shares tendered—not such a good deal. The Beatles' offer involved cash to the tune of 2.1 million pounds, of which

149

Ansbachers was putting up about 1.2 million. None of the Beatles had the resources to mount a bid of this size alone. The two richest, John and Paul, could have used their Northern shares as collateral, but Paul would not commit his shares.

The necessary security had to be packaged. Maclen (Music) was good for 575,000 pounds, and Subafilms, owning rights to *A Hard Day's Night, Help* and *Yellow Submarine,* was down for 350,000. John's shares in Northern were worth some 1.1 million pounds and constituted the only remaining piece of collateral which the Beatles could readily summon. Allen Klein came up with the final piece of the jigsaw. He put up 45,000 Metro-Goldwyn-Mayer shares, held through his company ABKCO Industries, Inc., then worth about 640,000 pounds.

Klein had been the target of a very hostile press. Although he and the Beatles emphasized that he had no intention of joining the Northern board, and that neither he nor his company ABKCO would have any equity holding in the company, fears persisted that if the Beatles gained control, "this American" would be calling all the shots from behind the scenes. If neither Klein nor the Beatles intended to manage Northern, where then was the business acumen going to come from? "Uncle" Dick James had lost favor, and would most assuredly be out. As shareholders were not selling their entire holdings to the Beatles, they had a right to ask.

On April twenty-eighth, Allen Klein called a press conference at Apple in an attempt to try to pacify his critics. As the *Investors Chronicle* observed: "For unprintable language the conference must have set some kind of record in the City circles." Between the obscenities, Klein, wearing the inevitable polo-neck sweater and using the Harold Wilson trick of puffing at a pipe throughout the proceedings, said the assassination of his character was entirely beside the point. He could be the worst man in the world and it would have no bearing on the relative merits of the Beatles' bid in comparison with ATV's. Northern Songs would become "a wasting asset" under ATV. As for Northern's future management, the Beatles would elect music publisher David Platz, of Essex Music Group, to the board as managing director.

The next day, the Consortium of institutional shareholders declared its hand. It was about to stage a blocking operation in the Northern Songs' struggle. The Beatles got down to serious lobbying for public shareholders' acceptances. On April thirtieth, they splashed quarter-page ads in four national newspapers, promising their financial fans an extension of their song-writing services at Northern and noninterference with its management. Meanwhile, back at Warburg's, shrewd brains were trying to trip up the Consortium for the benefit of ATV. Warburgs, a first-league merchant bank particularly expert in bid situations, was determined to win this fight. Heading Operation Beatle at the bank was Arthur Winspear, a former financial journalist, and a tough negotiator with a brain that clings to detail.

Time was running out for ATV. Its offer was due to close on May second and only 1.8 million shares were in the bag. Sir Lew's corporation was in a tight spot. There was always a chance that the Consortium might whip its share certificates into the Beatles' hands, thus taking 212½ pence cash for nearly all its holdings and leaving ATV holding the baby.

After an emergency meeting at ATV House, an eleventh hour extension of ATV's offer was decided. ATV warned this time it meant business. If it had not obtained control by May fifteenth, it would return acceptances with thanks, and take up the Beatles' offer. At the beginning of the fight ATV had been adamant that it would not sell its shares "for anything." But as things warmed up the ATV strategy was continually to threaten to pull out and accept the Beatles' offer, leaving institutional and public shareholders locked in a Beatle-controlled company. In that event, ATV vowed, it would not be "a very firm holder" and would dispose of the remainder of its shares in the market, rather than sit on a large investment in a company it could not control. The effect on Northern's share price would be devastating, it warned.

Jack Gill, ATV's finance director, impressed the point upon the Consortium that ATV would sell out to the

Beatles if its own offer failed. The Consortium, though it suspected bluff, could not bank on it. Numerous attempts were made to get the City Takeover Panel—Britain's voluntary equivalent to the official Securities and Exchange Commission—to apply pressure to holding ATV to its word that it would sell to the Beatles. At least then everyone would know where he stood. But the panel took a passive line, ruling that ATV's position was perfectly clear and it saw no reason to intervene.

So the Consortium was on its own. As long as it remained united, it held the key to Northern Songs. By early May, however, certain members were growing tired of the situation and were looking for an easy solution. An all-out cash bid from ATV of, say, 165 pence a share would have swung it. ATV's Jack Gill dug his heels in and flatly refused the Consortium's proposal.

"They wanted cash and I didn't want to pay cash because I'd have had to offer it to everybody—including the Beatles." ATV did not want to buy "a wasting asset." Keeping the Beatles in Northern shares, or giving them ATV shares, was one way of safeguarding Northern's future prosperity.

Edgar Astaire says ATV's refusal to pay cash "put the boot in." It spurred the Consortium into action. And active it certainly was. It began working toward a coalition between institutional shareholders and the Beatles, who together would overpower ATV. The Consortium would vote with the Beatles to oust the Northern board and introduce new "independent" management. That done, neither the institutions nor the Beatles would have any direct voting power. All their shares would be placed until 1973 into a voting trust controlled by two independent trustees who were not directors of Northern. Such an agreement was hammered out over a series of meetings and talks at Ansbacher's, attended by key members of the Consortium and Mr. Ormrod. Neither Allen Klein nor any of the Beatles attended the meetings. But Mr. Ormrod thought it a reasonable deal.

It was decided that the new Northern board would comprise three approved representatives from each side, with David Platz as managing director. By that time the Consortium, too, had found itself a representative—the smooth and likeable Ian Gordon, managing director of Constellation Investments, an investment trust that has specialized in acquiring the future earnings of many of Britain's top entertainers. Gordon, it was felt, had a better chance than anyone of getting on with the Beatles, given his experience and genuine affinity for entertainers.

Mr. Gordon takes up the story: "Ormrod at this point was doing his level best to push this agreement through. It really came down to persuading John Lennon, who certainly dictated to the other two. Paul's position was not clear. He denied that Klein represented him, but I think he would have gone along with this deal because we seemed to be on good terms with his father-in-law, so that was all right. Then Lennon became downright obstructive. He grudgingly said I could be a member of the board, but he did not see why the Beatles should bother to take over a company and then be told they could not do what they liked with it. He said he would rather let Grade have it than be dictated to like this. This is where we all came to a grinding halt."

The agreement came so close to being signed that a press release had been prepared for May fourteenth—the day before ATV's offer was due to close. Now the only course left for the Consortium was to obstruct the ATV bid. The brokers and their clients gathered in Astaire's office the following day. As the afternoon wore on, it became apparent that ATV was not going to make it.

Later that evening—at about 7 P.M.—Edgar Astaire took the first step to making a deal with ATV. He telephoned Warburg's and offered to talk. But he was rebuffed. The Consortium was then in a tight spot. It realized that it had only one day and a weekend before Monday, when the Beatles' bid expired, in order to turn ATV into an ally. ATV was in no mood to make friends. Most of Friday passed in sulky silence. The bulk of the activity fell over the weekend. By that time, ATV had announced defeat to the world. Its offer for Northern had attracted acceptances totalling only forty-seven percent.

The scene switched to Edgar Astaire's house on Saturday, where a long series of telephone calls took place

153

between Warburg's and Astaire and back to other key members of the Consortium. The idea then was to make a deal with ATV to ensure that the Beatles did not get control on Monday. ATV did not trust the Consortium, arguing quite reasonably that a group of brokers could neither dictate to their clients nor speak with one voice for so many diverse interests. Any agreement with such a Consortium would not be legally binding. ATV wanted assurances, and yet more assurances. It wanted the signatures of everyone concerned on an agreement. It was no use haggling over the problem on the telephone, so they all agreed to meet at ATV House at three o'clock on Sunday afternoon.

Ian Gordon had been in the country. He turned up at about 7 P.M. to witness "one of the great classic scenes of the whole saga." By the time he arrived, the talks had moved to the L'Epée D'Or restaurant, at the Cumberland Hotel, and the negotiating knot already had the beginnings of a legally binding draft document. "We dined. And then we went on discussing. We went on and on and on and I think it finished at three o'clock in the morning.

"They had piled up the tables all round us. Everybody had gone home, only the night watchman was on. Edgar was lying on some piled-up tables, asleep. We others were in our shirtsleeves, bent over this scrap of paper. As everybody said, we were never going to get a bit of paper which was legally binding. It was really only there to show ATV that we wouldn't do the dirty on them."

The Beatles' bid was going to expire on May nineteenth, at three P.M. on a Monday afternoon. Members of the Consortium had to turn up at Warburg's offices at 2:30 P.M. and sign the agreement, committing all participating shareholders, or at least enough of them to ensure the Beatles could not win. The main points of the agreement were: 1) that over a period of twelve months neither party could sell its shares without prior consultation; 2) each party had the right of pre-emption; 3) Ian Gordon, representing the Consortium, would go on the Northern board; 4) the punch line: "Members of the Consortium undertake that during the currency of this agreement they will exercise their votes so as to maintain on the board of Northern Songs sufficient nominees of ATV to give them a majority."

In that last clause the Consortium signed effective control to ATV. Ironically, it very nearly did not happen. Back to Ian Gordon: "The first excitement of the day [Monday] was when I rang Slater Walker to make sure everything was all right. I was informed that Slater's had decided they were accepting the Beatles' bid. So my first call was at Slater's where, after a long talk, they reconsidered and said okay, they would go along with us. I thought that the panic was over, because everyone else was getting his bit done, but no. It turned out that Ebor Unit Trust had not agreed to sign. I learnt this while having lunch. So I went on a great chase through London to try and find Norman Miller of Ebor and get him to sign. I did eventually find him and I delivered another impassioned plea—it was then 2:25 P.M." Miller finally agreed.

"We went 'round with great speed—I mean still running —to Warburg's. Fortunately all these places were within yards of each other. At last we went into this room at Warburg's where this marvelous gathering was taking place —everybody eyeing everybody edgily. Nobody had been quite sure of how Triumph Investment Trust would operate and someone had been in charge of getting them. Suddenly somebody shouted 'Christ! What about Triumph?' and somebody else said 'It's all right, I've got them locked in the next room'—although I don't know whether that was actually true."

It wasn't. Triumph remained in splendid isolation throughout the deal.

"Then another panic. In all the excitement, another broker had forgotten to tell his clients not to accept the Beatles' bid. Everybody turned on him. He shot out and was seen sprinting down the road like the white rabbit in *Alice in Wonderland* trying to get to his clients before it was too late."

The broker's version is different: "I had one institutional client who had a messenger standing outside Ansbacher's door with the shares in his hand. Provided I could come out before three P.M. and say 'It's all right; we have signed with ATV,' he would not lodge them. But if the Consortium had fallen through—he would quickly nip into Ansbachers and hand his shares to the Beatles.

"There were tight deadlines and we kept on going over these bloody deadlines. The Beatles' offer closed at 3 o'clock and this thing was supposed to be signed at 2:30. I was there, but the whole Consortium was not. Everyone was late and then arguments were raised—it was utter chaos. Finally, at a few minutes to three, I said, 'Look, either we have a Consortium or we haven't. There is a messenger standing outside Ansbacher's with shares and I must stop him.' They said, 'We have a Consortium,' so then I said, 'Well I must go'—and I ran."

Whether the broker made it in time or not was irrelevant because the vast majority of the Consortium was there and so the deal was signed barely fifteen minutes before the Beatles' offer closed. ATV had effective control of Northern Songs.

Meanwhile, Allen Klein and the Beatles were all sweating it out in another room at Ansbacher's, unaware of the happenings of the night before or of the excitement just a few yards away. "Klein told me afterward that at that point they were deciding what to do with the company when they got control. They were arguing about who should be director," smiled Jack Gill.

The Beatles were back to square one, "Except that we owed Ansbachers 5,000 pounds," said John Lennon bitterly. On May twentieth, John and George trudged back to the City to see Sergeant Ormrod. They were depressed, disappointed and hostile towards ATV and its new allies. ATV lost no time moving its men onto the Northern Songs board. On May twenty-third it announced that Jack Gill would join as a director and so would Louis Benjamin, managing director of ATV's record offshoot, Pye. Silver would continue as chairman and James as managing director. Ian Gordon was to take a seat as representative of the Consortium's interests. ATV and the Consortium were sporting enough to invite the Beatles to nominate their own representative, but the invitation was ignored.

156

And so the action went underground. The London financial district lost interest, believing that defeat had crushed Klein and that the disenchanted Beatles were sulking somewhere abroad. It would only be a matter of time before the Consortium sold control to ATV, thus locking the talented songbirds in Sir Lew Grade's menagerie. Sir Lew would have liked nothing better than to control a company in which the Beatles were both the major assets and large minority shareholders. But it did not happen quite like that in the finale, some four months later.

Klein was not idle during this lull. Far from it. Shuttling back and forth from London to New York, he kept the Northern Songs' pot gently simmering while stirring the other meaty morsels of Beatle fortune, as Sir Joseph Lockwood of E.M.I. and Leonard Richenberg of Triumph Investment Trust will bear witness. The Beatles had unfinished business with both these gentlemen, and "Old Allen" was attending to it with his usual gusto.

With E.M.I., there was the matter of the Beatles' exclusive recording contract. The contract expires in 1976, but the boys had virtually fulfilled the minimum provision of five long-playing and five single records by 1969. So they were in a splendid bargaining position to demand more cash for future recordings. Klein's argument was no increased royalty, no more records. The rationale was crystal clear to E.M.I., which at the time was enjoying bumper Beatle sales in America, via Capitol, and throughout the rest of the world.

Throughout the months of negotiations at E.M.I.'s London headquarters and at Capitol's HQ in Hollywood, Klein laid down a very hard line which won the respect of E.M.I. executives. One said: "He is very good for his clients. Few people could have machinated that contract so well. He drives a very hard bargain, and though he is confusing to negotiate with, he's a very good businessman, there's no doubt about that."

Of course, Klein had every incentive to excel over the E.M.I. contract. He had to justify his presence to the Beatles, and in particular to John Lennon, who, having defended him in front of Paul's fervent opposition, was beginning to have quiet doubts that Klein was as good as he said. After all, he promised he could perform many feats, and had so far failed in two major initiatives—to get control of Northern Songs and to buy back Nems from Triumph.

The renegotiated terms of the E.M.I. contract gave the Beatles 25 percent of the wholesale price from American sales. The Beatles used to get 17½ percent of the wholesale in America—already a steep rate by industry standards. But then, the Beatles were special. Their records took more time—five to six months—and money—several thousand pounds—to produce, and unit by unit were less profitable than E.M.I. would care to admit. But what sales!

Back in September, 1969, Klein was boasting the detailed terms of the Beatles' new contract with Capitol. He said the increased royalties were subject to the Beatles fulfilling a minimum provision of two LPs a year until 1976 —either collectively or individually. If they did, all new albums would earn them fifty-eight cents each until 1972 and seventy-two cents from 1972 to 1976. That compared with six cents per album before 1966 and some thirty-nine cents from 1966 to 1969. Reissues of early recordings would attract a fifty-cent royalty per record until 1972, and seventy-two cents after that.

The contract marked a turning point in the relationship between Allen Klein and the Beatles. He had proved himself to all but Paul—although even Paul was happy to sign on the dotted line extended by E.M.I. after Klein's hard work.

But Klein was working hard on the Northern Songs front, too. First he made direct approaches to members of the Consortium with offers for their shares on a forward basis when their agreement with ATV expired in May 1970.

In August, the American brokerage house, A. J. Butler, Klein's old friend from the Cameo-Parkway days, who was now acting for the Beatles, made a cash offer of 165 pence a share for the Consortium's block in Northern. But the institutions would not play ball at that price. These and other "oblique approaches" were not taken seriously, according to one member of the Consortium.

"Americans are very different from us," he said. "They say they will make a bid, but really they are just staking their claim." As for Butler's proposal: "It was too low and we couldn't deal with them in any case because we had an arrangement with ATV and couldn't sell."

Klein turned to ATV.

"He came to see Sir Lew with vague terms under which he would see to it that we got control of Northern by delivering the Beatles' shares to us," said Jack Gill. "At that time he was there to knock the Consortium. The main concession was that Apple would get sub-publishing rights for the Beatles' songs throughout the United States and Canada.

"We were willing to consider it, but told Klein that we were not in a position to do so at that time, because of our agreement with the Consortium."

ATV was not happy. It wanted to finish what it had started and gain control of Northern Songs by buying out the brokers and their clients. But its own share price that summer was greatly depressed in a dull stock market and it also realized that to buy out the brokers would mean making another takeover offer to all shareholders, including the Beatles. That it wanted to avoid.

Then, early in September the Consortium started to fall apart. Private clients of Spencer Thornton wanted out. Alarmed at the new splash of headlines speculating about the future of Northern Songs, they decided to sell their shares while the going was good. David Galloway tried in vain to persuade them to hold on. He says he informed his colleagues in the Consortium as each selling operation was about to take place, giving them the option to buy the shares before they were put through the market. ATV bought some of the shares, sensing that a finale was near and it was time to go in for the kill.

"We thought we'd get their shares in the end," commented Jack Gill. "It was very difficult to deal with a Consortium of that nature—with so many different interests. Anyway what right has a broker to pledge his client's shares? If the client decided to sell that was that. The agreement meant nothing."

On September eighth, Jack Gill declared that ATV had increased its stake in Northern by some three percent, giving it a total of thirty-eight percent. The Consortium, realizing that the game was virtually over, decided to sell to ATV, but insisted on cash. "The price we had in the back of our minds was 212½ pence a share," said Edgar Astaire.

Peter Donald, chairman of Howard and Wyndham, had gone to see Sir Lew and Jack Gill and a price was agreed —200 pence a share for Howard and Wyndham's stake. But ATV insisted on all or nothing. Said Jack Gill: "Peter Donald agreed to sell his shares to us at that price and said he would try to get the others to agree to do the same. We agreed on terms that they should all accept, or the whole deal was off."

Everyone gathered in Astaire's office. They all agreed to sell, and a phone call to Warburg's settled it. On Friday, September nineteenth, ATV bought enough Northern shares from the Consortium to build its own stake up to just under fifty percent. Klein and the Beatles no longer had the remotest chance of gaining control of Northern.

But Klein was determined to salvage what he could from the Beatles' failed bid. By that time he and Sir Lew had come to understand each other perfectly. "They got on like a house on fire and had respect for each other in business," said Jack Gill. So Klein called on Sir Lew almost immediately after ATV had claimed victory in the fight for Northern Songs, and started negotiations, hoping he and the Beatles would be winners in the final round.

The broad lines of the ATV-Beatle argeement negotiated by Klein were that: (1) ATV would buy all their Northern shares in exchange for loan stock and cash; (2) The Beatles would withdraw the outstanding writs lodged against Northern Songs by Maclen (Music); (3) John and Paul would re-sign as songwriters until 1976—and George and Ringo would switch from Apple Publishing to Northern, also until 1976; (4) Lenmac would be sold back to John Lennon and Paul McCartney, and (5) Apple would get sub-publishing rights in the United States.

"We all finally agreed," said Jack Gill with a sigh. "It was a very good deal for both sides. Heads of the agreement were drawn up with our respective lawyers. Then, Allen Klein couldn't get the Eastmans and Paul to agree and so it fell through.

"John and Lee Eastman had stopped the deal. They wouldn't let Paul be a party to an agreement negotiated by Klein on behalf of all the Beatles. There was no way the two Beatle factions could agree.

"Klein was very sorry and I was very sorry because part of the deal was that we'd have got Harrison and Ringo, who at the time really didn't mean much. Of course, George Harrison has since been a great success as a songwriter."

"I can't understand it to this day," observed Sir Lew. "They [the Eastmans and McCartney] were mad not to take ATV shares considering what they'd have been getting."

So it was time for the Beatles to move their final counter; to sell their shares in Northern to ATV, since they did not wish to retain their holdings under the aegis of Sir Lew's corporation. ATV did not want to buy them out. From its point of view, the Beatles' stake in Northern represented an anchor to secure the company's future profitability.

However, ATV had bought out the Consortium for 200 pence cash a share and now the City Takeover Panel and other London financial eminences were demanding that the same offer be extended to the Beatles and other minority shareholders. There were panic calls from the Bank of England to Warburg's when it was learned that Jack Gill had no intention of buying the Beatles out.

Klein claims credit for "forcing Sir Lew to bid 200 pence." "The panel was evidently going to stick by its guns," he said. "It was the smart thing to do."

"What were they going to do about it? What could they have done?" said Gill. "I personally would have held out because I think it was in the interests of ATV shareholders that the Beatles stay locked in Northern. We would not have this mess of writs right now if they had. The panel is supposed to protect shareholders, but in this case, it was trying to protect two individuals—Lennon and Mc-Cartney."

The ATV board and their advisers at Warburgs didn't really want to bring the panel down on its knees. "We said, all right, we'll bid," said Gill, "but not cash. Eventually the panel said okay, so long as you make an offer."

The Beatles got ATV loan stock for their shares. Sir Lew fears they have now sold all this stock. Earlier hopes of extending their song-writing contracts are dead. "But I take the view that the songs in Northern already will live on forever."

The saga had continued for more than six months. The song-writing team of John Lennon and Paul McCartney had not been operating for some time before the battle began, but their relationship had been ruptured even further by the hair-raising proceedings. Paul had turned for advice to his father-in-law Lee Eastman and brother-in-law John, while Lennon and the others listened to Allen Klein.

Nearly two years after ATV's acquisition of Northern, the writs were still flying. Linda Eastman, who, according to Jack Gill, "never wrote music before her marriage," became the center of a legal row between ATV and Paul McCartney. McCartney insisted that she helped him write "Another Day," and other compositions. He claimed her entitlement to half the copyright earnings.

Remarked one member of the City Consortium who was pleased to get out of Northern before the legal rows blew up: "All it needs now is for the kid [Linda Eastman's daughter, Heather] to take up the piano."

CHAPTER NINE

The Long and Winding Road Through the English Courts

Both John Lennon and Paul McCartney were married within a few days of each other in March 1969. Subsequently, there took place an astonishing reversal of roles. The Beatle who had always scorned blatant publicity hunting was now married to one of the world's most talented publicists. When the businessmen of London started snapping like piranha fish at any exposed part of the Beatle fortune, John and his new wife coolly divested themselves of their clothes, making sure that their names wouldn't appear only on the financial pages. John began to actively seek the headlines with every conceivable outrage, many of which were undoubtedly dreamed up by Yoko. In contrast, Paul McCartney, though still skilled at maintaining good public relations, as he later proved, seemed to lose interest in the public domain and retired to his farm in Scotland. He secluded himself so successfully that by the fall of 1969, a rumor that he was dead had circulated throughout the United States and found many millions of believers.

Although the Lennons spent many hours that spring hobnobbing with London's merchant bankers, they appeared to most of the world as a pair of peace fawns. Dressed all in white, they were married in Gibraltar, and to the delight of the European glossies, made their honeymoon a public event with a bed-in at the Amsterdam Hilton. John told newsmen from the crumpled bed linen: "Everything we do we shall do together. . . . I don't mean I shall break up the Beatles or anything, but we want to share everything." It was a remark so typical of John Lennon, who has made a habit of speaking first and thinking afterward.

After liberating the Netherlands, John and Yoko chose Vienna as their bastion for expounding a philosophy of total communication, love and peace from the inside of an outsize pillow case. Their credibility about total commitment to such noble sentiments was rather badly damaged a few days later, when they scurried back to London to devote their attentions to such a mundane matter as the prospective takeover of a music publishing company.

When business had been taken care of, they took up their noble sentiments again and planned an invasion of the United States. Unfortunately, this was thwarted by the cancellation of Lennon's U.S. visa. John had been convicted of marijuana possession a few months earlier, and not even a bombardment of "acorns for peace" and "war is over" posters could convince the little gray men of the State Department to change their minds. So the invasion was halted at the United States' border, in the staid city of Toronto, where Lennon preached his peace philosophies to radio stations throughout the United States from his hotel room phone. He even invited Canada's Prime Minister, Pierre Trudeau, to join him in a bed-in, or at least to meet with him to receive an acorn. Trudeau very cautiously declared: "I don't know about acorns, but if he's around I'd like to meet him. He's a good poet." The Lennons were given an audience six months later by the Canadian Prime Minister when John was making arrangements for the abortive Toronto Peace Festival. They found him "more beautiful" than they expected, and have since regarded him as their number-one fan.

John and Yoko decided to emphasize their togetherness through their records. "Two Virgins" was followed by "Unfinished Music No. 2, Life with the Lions" and, eight months after the event, they issued a "Wedding Album." By this time, they were well on their way to rivaling Richard Burton and Liz Taylor for the title of world's biggest bores, but still the avid publicity seeking didn't stop. Lennon decided it was time to end the four years of torment which he had endured since accepting an M.B.E., even though the medal had been lying undisturbed on his Aunt Mimi's television set for most of the time. His reasons for returning the award, he explained, were to protest British involvement in the Nigeria-Biafra confrontation and Britain's tacit support of American actions in Vietnam. He also used the opportunity to complain that his single "Cold Turkey" was slipping down the charts. A few months later, Lennon proclaimed that the Beatles had smoked a joint in the toilets of Buckingham Palace before accepting their M.B.E.s from the Queen. The British cartoonist, Giles, produced a hilarious sketch of police with trained dogs raiding the royal household, but the controversial statement drew only a typically restrained comment from a Palace spokesman.

"Obviously, when people come along to investitures, toilet facilities are available," he said grittily.

Some of Lennon's actions at this time were certainly well motivated. He paid fines totalling over 1,000 pounds for all demonstrators arrested during a protest against the South African rugby team's tour of Britain. But nothing was ever enacted without an accompanying barrage of publicity, and Lennon was always on somebody's front page.

However, the lack of any mention of McCartney in the press prompted the amazingly rapid dispersal of a rumor that he was dead. In the fall of 1969, it swept through the United States, coinciding with the release of the "Abbey Road" album. This only fueled the gossip even more, because Paul appeared on the jacket with his eyes closed and in bare feet, supposedly signifying that he had risen from the grave. Also on the album cover was a yellow Volkswagen bearing the license plate "28 IF." This was widely interpreted as a subtle suggestion from the other three Beatles that Paul would have been twenty-eight, if he had lived. Nobody ever quite discovered where the death rumor originated. A Michigan student took credit for making a detailed analysis of all the "clues," and concluding that Paul had been killed in a car crash in 1966. But it was Detroit disc jockey, Russ Gibb, who first brought the rumor to the air waves. A number of other Midwestern DJs followed his lead and soon the entire youth of the country was talking about it.

Although nobody accused Capitol Records, ABKCO Industries or any of the Beatles of starting the myth, no great pains were taken to quash it as quickly as possible. Not surprisingly. Sales of "Abbey Road" were soaring, there being nothing like death to stimulate demand for an artist's work. Stores throughout the country reported increased buying, not only of "Abbey Road," but of earlier Beatle LPs as well. One store even took display ads in the daily papers, offering the last six Beatle albums in a kind of "funeral" package. Eventually, "Abbey Road" sold more than five million copies, over a million copies more than any other Beatle album either before or since. No wonder Allen Klein was smiling.

"Abbey Road" was the last album the Beatles were to record together, but it was not the last Beatle record to be released. "Let It Be" had been recorded back in the winter of 1969, in a cold, inhospitable studio at Twickenham. This was the low point of the Beatles' recording career. The presence of film cameras only contributed to the tensions between them, and the album was finally abandoned and lay fallow until the spring of 1970. Even before "Let It Be," the Beatles had had serious disputes with each other, following differences of opinion about music. For the most part, these had been settled fairly amicably, but the arguments about "Let It Be" were never settled. They figured prominently in the affidavits of each Beatle when Paul McCartney sought a dissolution of the Beatles and Co. partnership in the English courts. Derek Taylor emphasizes that although John and Paul had by this time developed markedly different attitudes on many issues, and were feuding about prospective managers, there appeared to be an ever-widening gap in their musical inclinations.

Oddly enough, Ringo was the first dissident Beatle. While the "White Album" was being recorded late in 1968, Ringo announced he was leaving the group. He returned within a few days.

"I felt tired and discouraged . . . took a week's holiday, and when I came back to work everything was all right again," he said. However, he added some harsh words about Paul. "Paul is the greatest bass guitar player in the world. But he is also very determined; he goes on and on to see if he can get his own way. While that may be a virtue, it did mean that musical disagreements inevitably arose from time to time."

Friends say Paul had been nagging Ringo for some time about his drumming. Paul is himself an excellent drummer and Ringo had begun to feel redundant. Paul felt slightly guilty for having been too authoritarian and Ringo came back to the studio to find his drums smothered in flowers.

George was the next to walk out. Although Paul claims that George had argued with all three of them, George insists his row was exclusively with Paul. The quiet Beatle had been composing many more songs since the group had ceased touring. He had just returned from the States where he had played casually with many leading musicians in a very relaxed, cooperative atmosphere.

"This cooperation contrasted dramatically with the superior attitude which for years Paul had shown towards me musically," George explained. "In normal circumstances I had not let this attitude bother me and to get a peaceful life I had always let him have his own way, even when this meant that songs which I had composed were not being recorded.

"When I came back from the United States . . . I was

167

in a very happy frame of mind, but I quickly discovered that I was up against the same old Paul. . . . In front of the cameras, as we were actually being filmed, Paul started to 'get at' me about the way I was playing."

After the row, George felt that Paul treated him more as a musical equal. Until this time, McCartney had selfishly demanded most of the attention, and regarded only John as his equal. George had lacked self-confidence, but now he was beginning to stand up for himself and realize his full potential as a songwriter. However, it wasn't until the release of "Abbey Road" that his two songs "Here Comes the Sun" and "Something" established his reputation in this capacity.

It was the next resignation that really finished the Beatles as a group. After "Abbey Road" was released, Paul McCartney, who contrary to popular opinion was very much alive, proposed that the group should play live before small audiences. Paul's idea was that the Beatles would be billed under an assumed name, and they would simply show up and play. In spite of the bickerings about music and the eight months of feuding between Klein and the Eastmans, McCartney at this time still thought of himself as a Beatle and wanted the group to continue. It was Lennon who decided that this state of not-so-peaceful co-existence had gone on long enough. He told a stunned McCartney that he wanted a divorce. It was agreed that nobody should know the group was finished; the divorce would be kept out of the papers. For this reason, the other three felt betrayed when eight months later McCartney blew a fanfare to announce that *he* was leaving. "As far as Paul was concerned, John's request for a divorce was the final break," said John Eastman.

Ironically, John Lennon, the Beatle who asked for a divorce, went to great lengths in court to emphasize that the musical marriage had not worsened over recent years. Lennon contended that during the making of the "White Album" in 1968, musical differences between him and Paul were not more marked than before. He denied that the Beatles were becoming "musically less compatible."

"We were no more openly critical of each other's music in 1968, or later, than we had always been," he said. "I do not agree [with Paul] that after the touring ceased we began to drift apart socially and that the drift became more marked after Brian Epstein's death."

McCartney pounced on the comment in one of his court affidavits.* While Paul had been quietly preparing to serve his writ, requesting the dissolution of the partnership, the unfortunate Lennon had been sounding off in his usual, flamboyant way in a *Rolling Stone* interview. Paul pointed out that John's remarks in his affidavit were diametrically opposed to his statements in the interview.

A full eight months elapsed from the time Lennon asked for his divorce until Paul issued his headline-making resignation. Lennon was furious that he hadn't done what Paul did, because it sounded as if Paul was the only dissatisfied party. Paul claimed that the idea that he would leave gradually formed in his head when he was recording his first solo album "McCartney." But there was certainly more to Paul's resignation than simply the formation of an idea in his head. He was bitterly offended that he'd been asked to postpone the release of his solo album, so that it wouldn't coincide with the release of the group effort, "Let It Be."

The dispute over these album release dates was probably the main reason for Paul deciding a few months later that he wanted to leave the partnership. Although John Eastman claims that it was Paul's concern over his tax position that prompted him to serve his writ, there is little doubt that after his experience with the LP "McCartney," Paul envisioned further obstructions to his career as a solo artist. He had also asked Lennon about a possible dissolution of the partnership long before the tax problem came up.

Paul claimed that he telephoned United Artists and was told that no release date had been fixed for the film *Let It Be*. He said Ringo had told him that the others would let his album come out if he agreed to a deal concerning the film.

* All affidavits referred to in this chapter were filed in the English High Court of Justice, Chancery Division, in the case of *Paul McCartney* vs. *John Lennon, George Harrison, Richard Starkey and Apple Corps Ltd.*

"At this stage Ringo also visited me," said Paul, "bringing two letters signed by George and John with which he said he agreed. These letters confirmed that my record had been stopped.

"I really got angry when Ringo told me that Klein had told him my record was not ready and that he had a release date for the 'Let It Be' album. I knew both of these alleged statements were untrue and I said in effect this was the last straw and 'If you drag me down, I'll drag you down.' What I meant was anything you [i.e. the rest of the group] do to me, I will do to you."

Paul McCartney's graceful St. John's Wood house had rarely witnessed an angrier scene. Ringo had been sent over to sort things out because only he still maintained a reasonable relationship with Paul. He expected Paul to be disappointed and therefore felt it was right that one of the Beatles should tell him personally. He was surprised when Paul exploded.

"To my dismay, he went completely out of control, shouting at me, prodding his fingers toward my face, saying 'I'll finish you all now' and 'you'll pay,' " said Ringo. "He told me to put my coat on and get out. . . . While I thought Paul had behaved a bit like a spoiled child, I could see that the release date of his record had a gigantic emotional significance for him. Whether he was right or wrong to be so emotional, I felt that since he was our friend and since the date was of such immense significance to him, we should let him have his own way."

By now the two sides were lining up to do battle. The other three Beatles and Klein were annoyed, to say the least, that sales of "Let It Be" would suffer because McCartney's solo album was being released at the same time. They felt "Let It Be" had been delayed long enough and they claimed they hadn't had a chance to even hear Paul's album. "The facts speak for themselves as far as I'm concerned," said Klein. "The film came out, didn't it? We wanted to hold back McCartney's album, but Eastman had already bought the trade advertisements for the album in America."

McCartney's second, John Eastman, was always at his shoulder during this bout, now playing a greater role in the drama, having sensed it was time for a showdown. Eastman says he discovered the record had been stopped while checking out certain details about the jacket. "I brought the tapes back to the States and told Capitol Records if they didn't put it out, Columbia Records would," said a defiant Eastman. "Apple had the right of approval, but Klein and the other three backed down."

The "Let It Be" saga, however, didn't end with the release of Paul's album. Klein had hired record producer Phil Spector to remix "Let It Be." Spector has always had a fondness for lots of lush strings, female voices and horns, a formula that made him a rock 'n' roll millionaire at a tender age, when it was applied to the voices of the Ronnettes and the Righteous Brothers. The same treatment was given to Paul McCartney's "The Long and Winding Road," but Paul wasn't impressed. When he received the acetate copy of the album, he wanted several changes made. He claims he was unable to contact Spector, but told the other three Beatles and Klein of his requests.

Paul, however, may have been having trouble making up his mind. He admitted that when he first heard the remixed album, he did okay it, because the others were so enthusiastic about it that he thought he might have been mistaken. One incredible statement in his affidavit read that his approval was made "in a tone of voice to convey that I understood their point of view rather than I agreed to it." The other three Beatles' lawyers probably are still trying to puzzle out what that particular statement meant. Paul claimed he later made strong representations to have the album altered and that there was plenty of time to make the changes. The others said Paul was too late notifying Allen Klein about the alterations he wanted. McCartney might have had his own way with his solo album's release date, but "Let It Be" went out as Spector had remixed it. Paul's pleas went unheeded.

"If Paul had wanted to make any changes he could have done so," said Lennon. "A complete track could be redone in two or three hours and the whole album in two or three days. In fact, there was at least a fortnight available before production needed to start, but so far as

I know Paul did nothing except write to Klein when it was too late."

The era of Beatle music had ended. Bored with their work, niggling at each other, it would have been difficult for the four Beatles to have been in the same room together at this time without an argument developing, let alone in a recording studio. But musical differences constituted only one of the battles in which the other three Beatles were embroiled with McCartney. Justice Stamp, in delivering a long opinion prior to appointing a receiver to take charge of the Beatles and Co. partnership, made only passing reference to the music disputes. He merely noted that Lennon had stated he was leaving the group several months before McCartney adopted a similar course of action.

"Confidence is gone," Stamp declared, "and although the discontinuance of joint recordings . . . is not in theory destructive to the partnership, it may be thought as a practical matter that it would be inequitable to do otherwise than dissolve it."

Stamp may have paid only scant attention to the music disputes, but he went into great detail about the management quarrels and other differences of opinion. He concentrated very heavily on the stocky little figure in his courtroom, who had diplomatically discarded his leisure outfits for a suit, and who sat quietly, unable to defend himself against allegations about his conduct, because he was not a party to the action. As Justice Stamp put it: "The controversy in this action centers around the personality and the activities of Mr. Klein."

Usually it takes two to start a fight, but for some inexplicable reason, Stamp confined himself almost completely to the role played by only one of the parties. He largely ignored the personalities and activities of the Eastman family, which, aside from the fact that they were relevant to the case, would have made equally interesting reading.

Paul McCartney had backed his case for the appointment of a receiver with four main arguments. He declared that the Beatles had long since ceased to perform as a group; that his artistic freedom was liable to be interfered with so long as the partnership continued; that no partnership accounts had been prepared since the Beatles entered into a deed of partnership in April 1967; that the other three Beatles had sought to impose upon him a manager whom he found unacceptable.

Although his writ wasn't served until December 1970, as early as the previous summer he had decided that he wanted to leave the partnership. John Eastman had sent Klein a biting letter in June.* It read:

> Dear Allen: I have written eminent tax counsel in London for an opinion on the suggested dissolution of the partnership. It would be helpful if you too would secure an opinion. I suggest you put your fertile mind to work on all the aspects. Obviously, it would be a fine achievement for us if we can work this matter out happily.

The letter produced no results. Allen Klein did not feel like putting his fertile mind to work for John Eastman. So Paul wrote to John in August, suggesting that they should "let each other out of the trap." John sent back a photograph of himself and Yoko, with a balloon coming out of his mouth, in which was written the caption "How and why?" Paul replied with a letter which read: *"How* by signing a paper which says we hereby dissolve the partnership. *Why* because there is no partnership." John sent Paul a card which read: "Get well soon. Get the other signatures and I will think about it."

McCartney and Eastman, however, took no action until November, when the British tax authorities wanted to know a little about the Beatles' earnings. Eastman admits he had been building a case, but claims it was the revenue's writ against the Beatles for failure to file their taxes that triggered them (Eastman and McCartney) into action, to begin proceedings to wind up the partnership. After the receiver was appointed, Paul broke a long self-imposed silence and explained how painful this action was.

---

* Letter submitted before the English High Court of Justice, Chancery Division, in the case of *Paul McCartney* vs. *John Lennon, George Harrison, Richard Starkey and Apple Corps Ltd.*

The traumatic decision rambled across several pages of *Life* Magazine, and was perfectly calculated to preserve Paul's image of a decent, considerate nice-guy. It was widely regarded in New York's more informed rock circles as perhaps the finest specimen of public-relations oriented garbage ever to spill onto the pages of a glossy. Paul told how the final decision to serve the writ was taken during a long walk through the Scottish Loch country with his brother-in-law, John Eastman. "We'd been searching our souls. Was there any other way?" Paul asked poignantly.

Lee Eastman's explanation was equally poignant. "Paul didn't want to do it, obviously," he said. "Yet the accounts were in such dreadful shape. It took a lot of courage on his part. He kept putting off the decision because it hurt him so much to do it. It was a heart-rending decision for him. Only the greatest provocation made him do it."

John Eastman was more direct. He regarded it as a great triumph for the forces of good over evil.

"Klein didn't know the writ was coming," he declared proudly. "He thought I was stupid and that Paul was chicken-shit. My philosophy has always been that an artist should own himself one hundred percent. Paul's position had become untenable. He was worried about his tax position and he had a choice between possible bankruptcy and Klein for seven years as a manager, or serve a writ.

"Klein is like a shark, he's totally illogical. He's a great salesman who could even sell iceboxes to the Eskimos, but he's the biggest bullshitter ever."

Paul's dislike for Klein, evident from their very first meeting, had certainly been intensified by prolonged exposure to the Eastmans. Broadway Allen had long ago given up hope of winning McCartney's respect, even as a businessman. By now, Paul was safely locked in the Eastmans' arms. Their office, after all, was between Fifth and Sixth avenues, a consideration that John Lennon says Paul believed to be a factor in the Eastmans' favor when the Beatles were trying to select a new manager. Paul had come a long way since he left his brief employment with a Liverpool trucking firm. He evidently recognized Picassos when he saw them. Furthermore, their owners were two charming lawyers, who undoubtedly didn't smother their steaks in tomato ketchup.

When Lennon introduced Klein to the Beatles, John Eastman had already been acting for the group for about a month. Lennon had not been impressed with him. He says in his court affidavit that Eastman gave him the impression of being an inexperienced, somewhat excitable and easily confused young man.

"We all knew of Paul's friendship with the family and it was in March 1969 [two months after Klein's arrival] that Paul and Linda Eastman were married," says Lennon. "I was against the idea of having as manager anyone in such a close relationship with any particular Beatle, but apart from that, they did not strike us as having the right experience or knowledge for the job which had to be done."

Klein was obviously a man with much more experience of the hurly-burly pop music business. Paul realized immediately that the new contender was a force to be reckoned with. He admits he gave Klein little opportunity to present his credentials. He even walked out of their first meeting, and according to Klein, telephoned John Eastman in New York to ask him to come to London for a future meeting.

McCartney says he distrusted Klein in view of his alleged bad reputation and he wanted the Eastmans to handle his affairs. He claims he was most anxious not to stand out against the wishes of the other three "except on proper grounds." He therefore thought it right to take part in discussions concerning the possible appointment of Klein, though he did not in the least want him as his manager.

For somebody who claims to have been so repulsed by Allen Klein, Paul McCartney was nevertheless quite prepared to reap a lot of the benefits of Klein's hard work. For nearly a year, he quite happily sat on the fence. When things went well and Klein secured good deals, Paul promptly placed his signature on the dotted line. When he felt things were not going his way, or were not to his liking, he ran to the open arms of the Eastmans, who were only too delighted to have the opportunity to denounce Allen Klein as a terrible person.

Klein lists numerous occasions in 1969 when Paul not only cooperated with him, but actively sought his help, or at least agreed that Klein should represent him. McCartney confirmed that he agreed to Klein looking into the financial status of Apple and the Beatles. According to Klein, there were many other occasions when he acted for Paul.

Paul was party to, and agreed with, the decision to terminate the arrangement whereby Nems collected royalties on behalf of the Beatles, the decision which caused Leonard Richenberg so much bother. Paul's signature is on the letter to E.M.I. notifying the company of the intended change of plan. Klein says McCartney also went along with the collective decision that only he (Klein) should have the authority to negotiate contracts with E.M.I. The talks took place directly with E.M.I.'s American subsidiary, Capitol Records, in the summer of 1969. When Klein obtained for the Beatles a whopping twenty-five percent royalty, McCartney readily signed the agreement. He also placed his signature on agreements submitted by E.M.I. dealing with recording rights throughout the world, other than in the United States and Canada, and on documents setting out who had the right to give all approvals to receive all payments under the various E.M.I. recording agreements. When Dick James and Charles Silver sold their Northern Songs shares to ATV, Klein claims Paul, as well as John, asked him to come to London to do something to counter the ATV bid. He says McCartney agreed to the preparation of offer documents, but then refused to allow his shares in Northern to stand as collateral security for the partial bid for the company. Klein pledged his own MGM shares in place of Paul's. In July 1969, Klein pulled off his settlement with Richenberg and Triumph, freeing the Beatles from Nems. He recalls Paul was the first to sign the agreement.

None of these claims by Klein were denied in Paul's affidavit. Nor did Justice Stamp say whether McCartney's attacks on Klein were altogether justified in view of this evident cooperation, although he did concede briefly that Paul had accepted the "product of ABKCO's activities."

Perhaps he did not consider it important. Certainly, Mc-
Cartney lined his wallet for some time because of Klein's
deals and some of the statements in Paul's affidavit make
little or no sense in light of this.

"As time went on, I grew increasingly to distrust Klein
on the grounds of his proneness to boast about his ability
to make spectacular deals which he proved unable to
fulfill," said Paul. "Part of my reason for not wishing
to have Klein as manager was based on what he failed to
do between the beginning of that year [1969] and May.
Klein told us, 'I'll get it [Nems] for nothing.' This is a
typical example of the exaggerated way Klein expressed
himself to us at this time, and it was because of matters
like this that I gradually became more and more determined that Klein was not the right man to be appointed
manager."

Klein admits he has a tendency to boast. "Sure I told
them I'd get Nems for nothing, there's no question about
that," he said. "But if the deals were so ba-ad, why did
McCartney agree to them?"

One very strong argument in Paul's favor in the court
case was that he never placed his name on the key document—Klein's management contract. Lennon says that
in the earliest talks between Klein and all four Beatles,
Klein made it clear to them what terms he wanted if
engaged as manager, and subject to alterations in detail,
these were the terms of the agreement the three signed
with him. He doesn't recall Paul making any objections to
the terms themselves. After four months of providing his
services to the group, Klein wanted a definite decision on
whether he was being given the job.

John says Paul kept putting off the others, making ex-
cuses and being unavailable if they tried to get in touch
with him. Early in May 1969, a proposed management
agreement was discussed by them all at a meeting with
counsel. McCartney said he wanted more time to consider;
John told him he'd had plenty of time. The other three
signed.

Apart from his mistrust of Klein and his dislike of
Klein's boasting, McCartney also felt that the New York
accountant tended to sow discord among them by playing

one off against the other. In his court affidavit, Paul gave one cutting example of this. He said Klein once told him on the phone: "You know why John is angry with you, it's because you came off better than he did in 'Let It Be.' The real trouble is Yoko, she's the one with ambition." Paul added that he often wondered what John would have said had he heard the remark. McCartney evidently understood that it is a wise tactic in war to have the enemy at each other's throats. Nothing upsets Lennon more than criticism of his wife.

Of course, the other three Beatles stated in their affidavits that it was the Eastmans who tried to stir up dissent. They viewed McCartney's in-laws as connivers, who not only wanted to handle legal matters for the group, but also take over its management. They didn't consider the Eastmans had the qualifications. Nor were they any too impressed with Lee Eastman's temperament.

Lennon recalled two occasions when he said Lee Eastman became "quite hysterical," screaming and shouting abuse at Klein. One was at Claridge's, the other at Apple in front of a merchant banker. He says it was because John and Lee Eastman would not cooperate with Klein and because they obstructed him that he and George decided to sack the Eastmans even as lawyers.

Klein had many examples of what he termed interference by the Eastmans in his business deals. When he was trying to arrange the movie deal with United Artists for *Let It Be,* Paul objected that the film could not be blown up satisfactorily from 16mm to 35mm. According to Klein's affidavit, this objection derived from advice obtained by Lee Eastman, who had consulted with another movie company. Lee wrote to an Apple employee, saying he had been advised that 16mm film was not suitable for motion picture usage. His argument was eventually washed down the drain. The 16mm film of *Let It Be* was quite suitable for film production, and as such proved a very profitable venture for the Beatles.

A few months earlier, Klein had secured the Nems settlement. After the deal, John Eastman wrote to all the Beatles, including Paul, saying that Klein had cost the group 1.5 million pounds. How he derived this figure, he didn't say in his letters, but Paul apparently felt the deal was sufficiently good to sign the agreement. When Klein began negotiations to revise the Beatles' recording contract terms, Eastman wrote Capitol, saying in effect that Klein had no right to represent McCartney, and that the deal would never be agreed to. When Klein delivered the goods, a vast increase in the Beatles' royalty, Eastman was forced to capitulate. Paul signed the contract.

In these instances, the Eastmans' involvement didn't foil Klein's plans, but in one very important case, it did. In the fall of 1969, Klein was trying to secure his agreement with ATV for the British entertainment complex to buy all the Beatles' shares in Northern Songs in exchange for ATV's own shares. Klein had agreed with ATV that Northern would get song-writing contracts with George and Ringo and that John and Paul's existing contracts would be extended beyond 1973, the year they were due to expire. In return Apple was to get the sub-publishing rights in the United States.

But before the deal could go through, Klein says he learned that ATV had received a letter from John Eastman stating that Klein had no authority to speak for McCartney. He claims that this was in spite of the fact that Paul had spoken on several occasions during the negotiations with ATV chairman, Sir Lew Grade, and had agreed with the proposals. According to Klein, Paul telephoned John Eastman in New York to find out why he had written in these terms to ATV. At the end of the conversation, he says, McCartney told Eastman not to send any more letters without first sending them to him for approval.

But Eastman's actions had shaken the confidence of the ATV board and the deal fell through.

"I thought the deal was crazy," said John Eastman. "I told each one of the Beatles, including Paul, that they could all fuck off if they went through with that deal. Paul was getting frightened by Klein's threats of ungodly tax problems if the deal didn't come off. My letter to Grade foiled Klein's plans."

Lee Eastman also claims the credit for stopping the deal.

"It wasn't so much John's letter as my call," he said. "I turned it [the deal] down. I called Grade and said, 'See here, we aren't extending the contract. Klein has no right to represent McCartney.'"

The Eastmans' comments didn't reach the ears of Justice Stamp. Since January 1969, they had loomed at Klein's shoulder. Their hostility toward him knew no bounds, yet in a thirty-four-page opinion Justice Stamp merely noted that McCartney and the Eastmans as allies "made Mr. Klein's task far more difficult than it otherwise would have been." He had nothing to add on the subject.

McCartney's final weapon against Klein was that no audited accounts for the Beatles had been placed in his hands. He claimed that Klein had promised to secure full, detailed accounts with respect to the Beatles' affairs at their first meetings. "But to this day I have not seen any accounts," Paul wailed.

Klein contended that the inability to finalize accounts was not due to shortcomings on the part of the staff of Apple or his own company, ABKCO, since it became manager in May 1969. He claimed that after Apple's accountant, John Chambers, left the company in August of that year, until the arrival of another accountant six months later, there was nobody available to take responsibility for dealing with audit questions. He said he was greatly preoccupied with other Beatles' affairs during this period. Draft accounts of the partnership were in fact delivered to McCartney only a few weeks after the writ was served on the last day in December 1970. Klein pointed out that if the records for 1970 had been in a bad state, it would have been impossible to produce even draft accounts so quickly.

January 1971 must have been a very busy month for Allen Klein. McCartney and the Eastmans had a head start with their writ. John Lennon was floating around in the Pacific, on his way to visit his Japanese relatives. "We were caught unprepared," Klein admitted. "Every time we put in an affidavit, they put in five."

By February the case was exploding across the headlines of the British papers: BEATLES' FIRM IN GRAVE STATE! PAUL IS A SPOILED CHILD—RINGO! BEATLES AND THE SPONGERS—BY LENNON. Things had certainly changed since the days of "All You Need Is Love."

Paul McCartney, sporting a full growth of beard, sat quietly in the front of the courtroom, holding hands with his wife Linda, while his lawyer, David Hirst, leveled his sights on Allen Klein. "Mr. Klein failed to keep proper accounts of the Beatles' affairs," Hirst charged. "He paid himself commission to which he is not entitled and is asserting his entitlement to even more. Mr. Klein cannot be trusted with the stewardship of partnership, property and assets. He has not cooperated with the accountants and there is ample evidence that the standard of bookkeeping is lamentable. The latest accounts suggest there is not enough in the kitty to meet even the individual Beatles' income tax and surtax liability, let alone the company's corporation tax."

An accountant with the firm employed by the Beatles disagreed. He said Klein had more than doubled the Beatles' income in his first nine months with the group and increased it by five times in 1970. The partnership's income had grown from 850,000 pounds for the year ended March 31, 1969, to 1,708,000 pounds in the nine months ended December 31, 1969. For the year 1970, the income was more than 4,350,000 pounds [$10,440,000]. "It is an odd kind of defunct business," commented the defense counsel, Morris Finer.

Klein was content to have his ability to make deals judged on his record. This, in itself, was quite impressive. He produced a schedule showing that the total income received by the Beatles from June 1962 until December 1968 (excluding income from song-writing, which was never part of the joint activities) was 7.8 million pounds. For the nineteen months since his management agreement took effect, total income was over nine million pounds. The amounts showed that Apple was perfectly solvent, said Mr. Finer.

On this point Justice Stamp was in agreement. There was evidence that the defendants had ample resources to meet their tax liabilities, he said. It was one of the few concessions he was prepared to make to the defendants in his opinion. Stamp placed considerable emphasis on the clauses of the deed of partnership signed by the Beatles in April 1967, when they were all taking LSD fairly heavily. He noted that the deed provided for the firm of Apple Corps Ltd. to manage the partnership, and appoint agents, distributors and licensees to carry out a number of other matters. These included obtaining engagements for the Beatles, exploiting the assets of the partnership and providing all necessary services. Then he turned his attention to the ABKCO management agreement drawn up by Klein. "A remarkable document," he called it. It read in part as follows:

Gentlemen: We hereby appoint you as our exclusive business manager under the following terms and conditions. I. Period: Three years (a) cancellable at the end of each year by either party giving three months written notice; and (b) cancellable by Apple if Allen Klein for any reason is no longer personally involved with the day to day details of running ABKCO.

II. Terms: (a) 20% of the gross commission received from any source during the currency of the agreement and 20% of all income whenever received as a result of all agreements signed during the currency of this agreement except as follows:

(i) amount of any Beatle record royalties arising from all existing record agreements, commission being payable only on amount of any increased royalty; . . .

The document was signed by John, George and Ringo and by Apple. Paul McCartney never signed it. Klein conceded that McCartney never accepted him as his manager, but claimed that the partnership did. Justice Stamp noted that the other three Beatles claimed the right to make what bargains they wished with Klein, without consulting McCartney. Paul, he said, was bound to concede that, according to the Partnership Act, any difference arising on ordinary matters connected with the partnership business may be decided by a majority. However, Paul had submitted that the appointment of Klein was not such a matter.

"The difference between the plaintiff and the defendants was not, in my judgment, as to an ordinary matter connected with the partnership," Stamp decided. "It was part of the contract between the partners that Apple should manage the business of the partnership. . . . By the appointment, if effective, Apple was displaced and ABKCO substituted."

The defendants claim, said the judge, that the ABKCO appointment could be supported under the clause of the partnership deed giving the company the right to appoint agents. "A manager is no doubt an agent," Stamp ruled, "but he is much more than that. The appointment of ABKCO without the concurrence of the plaintiff was, in my judgment, a breach of the terms of the partnership deed."

The other three Beatles had argued that it was also open to them to vary the terms of the ABKCO agreement without even telling McCartney. Stamp waved the claim aside, saying it effectively excluded Paul from the management of the partnership. He was very concerned, however, about the variation in the terms, and went into this in great detail.

"If the defendants' submissions [that they could vary the terms] were not well founded," said Stamp, "it must follow that sums of upwards of half a million pounds were, with their assent, wrongfully claimed by ABKCO as commission."

The judge evidently had spent many hours mulling over Klein's renegotiated agreement with E.M.I.'s American subsidiary, Capitol Records. The new agreement was a most complicated one. John Eastman might have called it the product of Allen Klein's fertile mind. It had made a bundle of money for the Beatles, but Stamp felt it had also made a bundle of money for Klein's company, ABKCO. Under its terms, E.M.I., owner of the Beatles' present and future recordings, granted a Beatle company,

Apple Corps Inc., the right to make and sell in North America any records from the recordings. Capitol's facilities were to be used for processing and pressing all records for Apple Corps in the United States, for which Apple would pay Capitol "x" dollars. The manufactured records would be distributed and sold by another branch of Capitol, which would buy the records from Apple Corps for "y" dollars. What reached Apple, or the Beatles through Apple Corps, was the amount by which "y" exceeded "x" dollars, known in the trade as the broker's turn. Stamp said the increase of payment to Apple, due to Klein's new deal, appeared to be equivalent to a royalty increase of 7½ percent. Then the learned judge brought down his ax.

"ABKCO has charged not twenty percent on the increase [as specified in Klein's appointment agreement] but twenty percent on the whole sum reaching Apple," Stamp declared. "The commission so charged amounts to 851,550 pounds, of which 647,572 pounds has been paid.

"It would be out of place to state with precision the excess of commission so charged over the amount chargeable under ABKCO's appointment," he continued. "It may be that the uplift of royalty exceeded 7½ percent. But on the figures before me, what has been charged is not less than three times the amount chargeable under the old agreement, and the excess is at least something over half a million pounds.

"I am quite satisfied . . . that subject to any alterations there may have been in the terms of the appointment, . . . ABKCO has made grossly excessive claims for commission, and has received commission grossly in excess of that specified in the appointment."

Klein had stated that the twenty percent commission had been charged on receipts after the deduction of pressing costs, mechanical royalties and E.M.I. royalties. In other words, he was saying that he had been decent enough not to take commission on the "x" dollars, while Stamp was already astounded that he had taken commission on the "y" dollars, let alone both.

"As I have said," Stamp continued, "the document by which the appointment of ABKCO was effected was in

truth a remarkable document. But if its legal effect was
that . . . ABKCO was entitled to commission, not only
on sums which Apple received from Apple Corps Inc.,
but also on the price paid by Apple Corps before deduction of the costs incurred in obtaining that price—to
have claimed that it would have had that effect would, in
my judgment, have been nothing more or less than dis-
honest."

One other paragraph in Klein's affidavit prompted Stamp
to launch a tirade against Klein and his lawyer. The paragraph read:

Schedule 2 shows what ABKCO has earned from
the beginning down to December 31, 1970. This is
strictly in accordance with the terms on which I insisted from the outset. There has never been any possibility of misunderstanding. Apart from personal
presents exchanged between individual Beatles and
myself, neither ABKCO nor I have received either
directly or indirectly any other benefits from our associations with the Beatles.

Stamp placed his tongue firmly in his cheek. McCartney's lawyer, David Hirst, had demonstrated that each
and every one of the "emphatic and unequivocal statements" in that paragraph, other than the first sentence,
was untrue, he said. Much time had been spent doing so.

"Mr. Finer, on behalf of the defendants, sought to
discount the effect of these untruths by dismissing the paragraph as a 'silly' paragraph, drawn per incuriam by some
draftsman in the late hours of the night," said Stamp
bitingly. "Everyone knew, he claimed, that it was a silly
statement, and he sought to criticize counsel for the plaintiff for taking so much trouble to demonstrate its untruth.
No doubt the plaintiff's advisers, when they read the papers, did know that the paragraph was false; but how the
judge could have known that, until it had been demonstrated or its falsity admitted, which it was not, I do not
know.

"The judge at the trial may have to decide whether the
statements made in paragraph 137 were in truth made

per incuriam, and speaking for myself, I have great sympathy for deponents to affidavits who are sought to be condemned on the strength of erroneous statements appearing in affidavits drawn by lawyers; but in paragraphs 125 and 137 of his affidavit, Mr. Klein is defending himself against a charge of taking unauthorized commission. If the paragraphs were not directed toward misleading the court into the belief that the commission charged was less—and less by many hundreds of thousands of pounds than might have been charged—the statements read to me like the irresponsible patter of a second-rate salesman."

The judge didn't relent on the subject of commission.

"It is a remarkable fact that neither in the affidavit of Mr. Lennon, nor in the affidavits of Messrs. Harrison and Starkey . . . is there the ghost of a suggestion that ABKCO's remuneration had been the subject of an agreement made after May 8, 1969," he declared. "On the subject of remuneration, Mr. Lennon simply says, 'So far as I know, he [Klein] . . . has not taken any commission to which he is not entitled."

Stamp found it "almost inconceivable" that had McCartney been informed of the alleged agreement, or had he been party or privy to the payments made following it, Klein would not have said so. He found it equally inconceivable that none of the individual defendants would not have referred to it.

"Moreover," said Stamp, "having regard to the relations between the plaintiff . . . and Mr. Klein, I entertain no doubt whatsoever that, had the agreement been brought to the attention of the plaintiff, there would have been a row. It would have reverberated through the voluminous mass of papers before me."

Stamp felt that the circumstances regarding the appointment of ABKCO and what he termed the subsequent surreptitious increase in its remuneration pointed clearly to the conclusion that the other three Beatles, either in conjunction with or at the instigation of Klein, were prepared to make the most important decisions without regard to McCartney's interests. The three individual defendants, he said, are adopting the position that they are entitled to overbear McCartney. Stamp rejected a submission by the defense counsel that if Lennon and Harrison, as Apple's directors, acted improperly in paying over Apple's money to ABKCO, then McCartney's only remedy was as a shareholder in Apple. He also threw out another submission that, in considering whether there ought to be a dissolution, the court would only treat McCartney as a partner to the extent of five percent. (Beatles and Co. being owned eighty percent by Apple, and five percent by each individual Beatle.)

"Apple is not . . . a Frankenstein set up to control the individual partners," said Stamp. "Equally do I reject what I think to be a fanciful notion—that there is some sort of analogy between the idea of democracy, enabling a majority to overrule a minority in the law of partnership. . . . Whatever powers may be conferred on a partner, he is bound not only to be just and faithful to his partners, but to render them full information of all things affecting the partnership.

"Apple, like the individual defendants, is the plaintiff's partner, and if, as is submitted, the defendants or any of them covertly made an oral agreement . . . increasing ABKCO's commission in the way I have indicated, without the plaintiff's knowledge and consent, it in my judgment committed a grave breach of its duties as the plaintiff's partner."

Stamp had given the newspapers plenty of front-page material on the Beatles' manager. Now he decided to be a little easier on Allen Klein.

"Mr. Klein is not on trial in this motion," he said. "I am sorry that he should have had to listen here day after day to allegations regarding his conduct, with which he, not being a party to the action, could not deal. I am sorry that the defendants did not in their affidavits make it clear that it was upon an agreement between them and Mr. Klein that they relied to justify the enormous payments made to ABKCO. It is a pity that he himself suggested that the payments made to him were within the terms on which he was appointed manager. Had it been otherwise, the attack on Mr. Klein would have been blunted.

"There is no evidence—and in view of the publicity

which has surrounded this case, it is right that I should say and emphasize this—that Mr. Klein has, without the knowledge of the defendants, put into his pocket any money belonging to the firm, or that he would do so. On the other hand, I must, in justice to the plaintiff, say that there are, in my judgment, grounds for his mistrust, grounds which may be dispersed wholly or partly at the hearing of this action, but nevertheless, in my judgment, prima facie solid grounds."

Having withdrawn the knife slightly, Stamp was now giving it another twist.

"There is the unfortunate fact that he [Klein] has been found guilty, and his evidence not believed, in a recent trial in New York on charges that he did unlawfully, wilfully and knowingly fail to make and file returns relating to the withholding of employees' taxes. It is right to add that the conviction is under appeal; but I find that Mr. Klein's description of the proceedings in his affidavit is somewhat disingenuous.

"Mr. Klein's affidavit does not persuade me that he was guilty of no impropriety in relation to the de-listing on the New York Stock Exchange of the company Cameo-Parkway Inc."

The learned Justice Stamp had made a big issue of a mistake in Klein's affidavit. Although it would have had no bearing on the outcome of the case, it would perhaps have been interesting to surmise what would have occurred if Klein had decided to make a big issue of this last comment by Stamp. First of all, Cameo-Parkway was never listed on the New York Stock Exchange; its shares were traded on the American Exchange. Stamp had earlier stated that he had "great sympathy for deponents to affidavits who are sought to be condemned on the strength of erroneous statements appearing in affidavits drawn by lawyers." Perhaps Klein had great sympathy for judges who might be condemned on the strength of erroneous statements appearing in their opinions, drawn by themselves.

Stamp, however, had turned his attention to the accounts.

"Until the eve of the issue of the writ, the plaintiff had

had no accounts of the partnership except some draft accounts for the sixteen months to March 31, 1968," said the judge. "Mr. Klein, according to Arthur Young and Company's evidence [the Beatles' accountants], was more interested in generating income than in the preparation of accounts.

"It is the defendants' case that the accounting in the office is better than it was, and it appears that the proper procedures were laid down early last year by the American representative of ABKCO, which, if followed, would in due course yield a satisfactory result. But unfortunately (to quote the words of Mr. Oldrey of the firm Arthur Young and Company), the principal defect of the procedure was that not all the staff concerned proved suitable or capable of implementing it.

"However successful Mr. Klein may have been in generating income, I am satisfied, on the evidence of the accountants and the accounts to which I am referred, that the financial situation is confused, uncertain and confusing. A receiver is, in my judgment, needed not merely to secure the assets, but so that there may be a firm hand to manage the business fairly as between the partners and to produce order. I have no doubt that a receiver and manager ought to be appointed.

"Whatever may have been the position when the motion was launched, serious attacks have been made, not only on Mr. Klein but on the bona fides of the plaintiff. I accept Mr. Hirst's [McCartney's counsel] submission that it is not reasonable to expect the plaintiff to submit to ABKCO's continued management.

"Mr. Klein remains the person with whom the plaintiff and his accountants have to deal. I accept Mr. Hirst's rhetorical submissions, 'How can the plaintiff, in light of his commercial trust and having regard to the inevitable personal difficulties that would arise, be expected to go on dealing with Mr. Klein?' dealing on matters of great personal importance to him, and dealing with matters of great commercial importance to him, because of the tremendous potentiality of his records."

Justice Stamp had evidently read his top forty.

"Nor do I believe," he said, "that the appointment of

a receiver will in the least degree discourage the purchase of Beatles' records from which their income stems."

With that the judge appointed a receiver. None of the Beatles were in court to hear the decision. Nor was Allen Klein. John Eastman placed a long distance call from a ski resort near Denver to learn the good news. Friends say when he came back to New York, he called many music business contacts and gloated: "Round one for the good guys."

"In my opinion, Stamp's judgment was very lucid and accurate," said John Eastman. "Especially when he referred to some of Klein's affidavit as the patter of a second-rate salesman. On the whole I feel it was a remarkable victory, to dissolve a partnership and get a receiver appointed for a five percent position. I have great faith in the English system of justice and the American system of justice for that matter.

"Klein's motives all along, I feel, were to make money for ABKCO. He had no artists worth anything at all if he didn't have the Beatles. Do you know what? Even now, Klein refuses to acknowledge that I have a brain in my head. He doesn't think I had anything to do with the lawsuit."

Klein denies that he doesn't give any credit to Eastman.

"Aw, that's bullshit," he snapped. "He did a helluva job, helluva job it was. Our people didn't know what was happening."

"They didn't think highly of Allen, 'cause he was an American and brash," Lennon interrupted.

"I couldn't understand the appointment of a receiver," sighed Klein. "If there hadn't been any money, then I could understand it, you betcha. But there's *so much money*. Yeah, the Eastmans won the round [concedingly], but the victory was mainly in PR. If you were Eastman, how would you explain to McCartney that it's not Apple that's in receivership, but Beatles and Company?"

Why didn't Allen Klein continue with his appeal of the receivership?

"The establishment, the establishment," sighed Klein ruefully. "It can always use discretion. I'm not too well liked in England."

And what did John Eastman think of it all? Did he consider that the entry of outsiders had intensified the differences brewing between the Beatles? Did he feel that he and Klein were responsible for hastening the breakup of the group?

Said John Eastman: "No, I never thought about it at all."

CHAPTER TEN

The Sum of the Four Parts
No Longer Equals the Whole

When Linda Eastman first introduced Paul to her family, Paul offered to play guitar for John Eastman's children. It was perhaps an omen to the future direction of his music. If John Eastman had been interested in Paul's music for its own sake, instead of attending to the dollars it could produce, he might have noticed something missing. Without the drive of John Lennon's rhythm guitar, Paul's recent lackluster tunes switched from the FM to the AM wavebands. His "Ram" LP, which he liked to regard as "Paul and Linda's downhome country album," according to publicist Tony Barrow, was little more than a collection of pretty jingles, lacking any substance. "Perfect car-driving music," one reviewer called it, amid a chorus of scorn from the underground papers. Paul hadn't lived up to their expectations.

In spite of the lawsuit to dissolve the Beatles' partnership, Paul McCartney still won sympathy from a wide cross-section of the public. On his album covers he was pictured alongside his wife and children, as if he wanted to be known as the family man of rock 'n' roll. He made no attempt to retaliate against the criticism from the underground. His albums might have been selling to a different audience than John's and George's, but they were still selling. A few months after Paul's "Ram" album was released, he announced that he was forming his own band. Its only other member of any renown was his wife Linda, a novice to the piano, but a legend backstage at the Fillmore East. Allen Klein described Paul as a musician whose ego was too great for him to tolerate a working association with a musical equal. On the other hand, Paul may simply have grown disillusioned with such relationships. He certainly severed many contacts with the rock scene. When he announced the formation of his band, the big-name impresarios were telephoning all over New York, trying to make contact with him. Paul, it seemed, had gone into seclusion yet again.

In contrast to Paul, John Lennon, aided and abetted by his volatile wife, continued to demand attention from the public. Sometimes his efforts cost him several thousand fans. Lennon has always been prone to outbursts of hostility. In recent years, these have been concentrated against any critics who dared to question either his wife's artistic merit or his own sincerity. In light of some of his actions, the latter might well be questioned. John once said he was extremely moved to hear people singing "Power to the People'" during a demonstration. According to one insider, John wrote the song because he was worried that he hadn't had a number-one single for a while, and thought "Power to the People" was a winner. Perhaps he had forgotten that.

John surrounded himself with the cream of rock musicians for his solo recordings. Billy Preston, Phil Spector and Eric Clapton were among the many who joined him in the studio, while Ringo and George also provided their services on several numbers. John claimed to write better songs and make better music without Paul, but although Paul may not have been in the studio with him, he was evidently still in the back of John's mind. Lennon's first album, he said, was about feeling his own pain. His second, by contrast, may have been intended to cause someone else some pain. Lennon wrote a song about Paul entitled "How Do You Sleep?" "It's real nasty," he said gleefully, forgetting that not so long ago he was all acorns and peace messages. But John Lennon can forget many things, very quickly.

The future looked bleak for Ringo Starr when the Beatles disbanded. He made two unfortunate attempts at solo albums, but suddenly came up with an excellent single. Although one of history's most charming bit-part players, he could never have hoped to occupy center stage in the pop music field. But Ringo, it seems, realizes that his future lies in films, possibly as a lead actor, and this time without the other three Beatles aiding him in a comedy routine.

As often happens, the strongest horse came from the back of the field. George Harrison had been writing many songs since 1966, tucking most of them under his pillow until the day he was no longer under the thumb of Commander Paul McCartney. His solo album "All Things Must Pass" won wider acclaim than any of the solo efforts by his more renowned former colleagues. Lennon says he feels George always labored under an inferiority complex. Nothing could have helped dispel that more quickly than the Madison Square Garden concert. George Harrison continues to be the most enigmatic Beatle, a man who warns "Beware of Maya," yet decorates his mansion with Tiffany lamps.

One inevitable question poses itself. Who was the most important and influential Beatle? The question can be argued ad infinitum. To begin with, the band was John's. He was the most ambitious Beatle in the early days, and much of the Beatles' early style, musical and otherwise, can be attributed to John's awareness. He knew what was good rock music and he showed an uncanny ability to draw from his own experience and relate it to others, either through his music or through his writing and humor. But John's interests moved away from the Beatles as a group, and Paul later gave the impression that it was he who was running things. Although Paul served the writ to dissolve the partnership, it was really Lennon who broke up the group, as much as it was he who formed it.

But the Beatles' phenomenal success resulted less from the particular contributions of any one individual than from the skillfully concocted group personality which they presented to the world. Each one had his little idiosyncrasies, and these, too, were offered for the amusement of the public. But the Beatles were always thought of as a group talent, and on their own they appear as stranded as one Marx Brother.

Whether they like it or not, they were immensely successful because Brian Epstein played down their individuality and made them seem like four parts of the same body, each with the same hairstyle, clothes and accent, all willing to be amusing at the same time, always on public display together. For a generation intent on escape and freedom, the Beatles seemed to point the way. The people whose tastes and habits they influenced now look at them incredulously, like children who have grown wise to their parents' weaknesses. Perhaps Brian Epstein, aware certainly of the flaws in the product he was marketing, saw the monster beginning to splinter in 1967 and realized that the myth would end. The Beatles themselves always seemed remarkably innocent with regard to the gigantic influence they exerted on both the entertainment business and youth in general. Their attempts to run a company exposed them as human beings to a generation that had previously regarded them as carefree gods.

As far as the Beatles' songs are concerned, most of them were written separately by John or Paul, although on some occasions they contributed bits to each other's compositions. A few were written with each contributing about equal proportions, often while on the road to an engagement. "From Me to You" was written in the back of a van. Generally, each takes the lead vocal in his own composition.

For a long time John questioned his own ability as a

song writer, and was beginning to have quiet doubts that he was as good as Paul, especially when McCartney came up with "Yesterday" and the song received such widespread critical acclaim. But both John and Paul seem to be endowed with a command for writing melody, and the decision as to who is better is a matter of personal preference. As examples, Paul wrote "All My Loving," "Yesterday," "Here, There and Everywhere" and, with the exception of the middle eight, "Michelle." John composed "In My Life," "Across the Universe" and "If I Fell." Their hard-rocking numbers again show no particular bias. "Please, Please Me" and "Day Tripper" were from John, "Paperback Writer" and "Lady Madonna" from Paul. But when they cooperated they almost invariably produced a smash hit—"She Loves You," "I Wanna Hold Your Hand," "Can't Buy Me Love" and "Day in the Life." However, by the time they were recording the "White Album" in 1968, they were no longer interested in co-writing, and the songs on that LP are all individual efforts. It was as if separate albums was the inevitable next step.

Some cooperation, if not as writers at least as recording artists, would probably have continued if the management dispute and the accompanying business battles hadn't occurred. The entry of such ambitious and bitterly opposed factions as Klein and the Eastmans brought the underlying differences to the surface. With John and Paul at loggerheads, the breakup was inevitable. Derek Taylor recalls John Lennon once storming around the Apple office, yelling "Fuck McCartney, that does it, I won't be writing any more songs with him." His annoyance, says Taylor, was over Paul's refusal to sign with Klein.

Allen Klein, however, a man who for some reason feels the need to disguise his humanity, has greatly aided George's solo career. Klein has often been described as a greedy, notoriously selfish individual, whose twinkling eyes grow even brighter at the sight of a dollar sign. "But he genuinely liked the Beatles from the first," said Derek Taylor, "even Paul."

It may be that since Klein acquired three Beatles, he has paid more attention to servicing his artists than he did in the past. Although he would never admit to it, perhaps he, too, has learned something from Brian Epstein's example. His three Beatles seem very satisfied with him. After all, he is making them money, and the importance of that commodity to them cannot be over-emphasized. But Beatles demand a lot of attention; they can be very difficult people to deal with in the long term. Brian Epstein's downfall can be explained by his inability to delegate his management to his working colleagues. He spent an inordinate amount of energy on Beatle matters. Allen Klein's organization is as much a one-man operation as Epstein's was. It may be no coincidence that he, too, is unwilling to delegate.

Lee Eastman, however, was only too willing to pass the responsibility for acquiring the Beatles to his son, John. For a man who is in the business of representing artists, Lee paid surprisingly little attention to keeping the Beatles together. Had he succeeded in representing them, he would have been able to bask in their reflected glory. They would have been as prominent trophies as the Picassos in his office. But Lee remained in the background, pushing forward his son to do battle with Allen Klein. When John Eastman proved no match for the persuasive powers of "Uncle Allen," in securing a majority of Beatles, Lee bared his teeth at the little New York accountant, but only succeeded in alienating the Beatles. When Klein's name was being bandied about in the English papers, and the British public was hearing the story of this terrible man who broke up the Beatles, Lee Eastman was not even mentioned. He was relaxing over a quiet game of tennis at his East Hampton home.

The story of the Beatles' breakup hasn't yet ended. Lennon and McCartney still communicate by telephone, though the conversations usually end in a shouting match, followed by a few weeks' silence and sulking. Nor have Eastman and Klein finished their battle. John Eastman determinedly says he plans to put Allen Klein out of business. After the receiver was appointed, Klein offered to buy out McCartney. He had received several offers for Apple from interested third parties, including his next-door neighbor on Broadway, Robert Stigwood. But Klein's intention was not to sell Apple.

He merely wanted to assure McCartney and the Eastmans that they were getting top dollar, because Klein
intended to top any bid with a dollar more.

"Paul wouldn't sell, though," says Klein. "Eastman came
to see me and said he wanted to buy." Stalemate. The
saga may yet continue back in the English courts.

For several years, the Beatles almost singlehandedly
directed the development of the recording industry. A
momentous organization such as E.M.I. was prepared, and
still is prepared, to bend over backward to please them.
Not for the sake of their art, though, but for the benefit
of the company's balance sheet. It took the slow-moving
wheels of the establishment a long time before they
caught up with the whirligig existence of the Beatles.
Then, the boys forgot about music as they were locked
at cross-purposes with big business. In light of this, "You
never give me your money" rang far truer than "All
You Need Is Love."

Rock music has been recognized as the most widely
acclaimed new art form of the sixties. It is paradoxical
that it has commercial organizations for its patron, which
are in no way motivated by art itself, but solely by the
profit accruing from mass sales. For artists such as the
Beatles, who wanted to communicate their music, whether
for commercial gain or not, there was no other outlet but
via the manufacturers of plastic, and the rest of the
grasping "entertainment" world. When they placed their
names on a recording contract, or a music publisher's
contract, they signed away much of their dignity. John
Lennon, hurrying back from Europe to take care of his
music publishing affairs, after its managers had stabbed
him in the back, was a much more undignified sight than
his public bed-in. The businessmen had at last got him in
their clutches. The Beatles had done the industry a great
favor. What had they received in return?

Surrounded by corporate thievery, it was no wonder
that they, too, became concerned if their wallets were
becoming a bit thinner. John Lennon, who once sang
"Turn off our mind, relax and float downstream," was

worried that he might end up bankrupt like Mickey Rooney. The Beatles' credibility had run its full course.

"The saviors," Derek Taylor once called them. Now *they* wanted to be saved. Paul, and to a lesser extent, George, slipped quietly toward the establishment. Lennon continues to feel that he is the most enlightened Beatle. For the most part, he snatches at whatever is topical and attaches his name to it. Ringo remains a true working-class hero.

The sixties produced charismatic figures in most walks of life. Many of their images have been tarnished as the truth about them surfaced in the cold, gray light of the seventies. The Beatles, charismatic figures in the field of pop music, met the same fate. The new era doesn't appear to be demanding superstars, and the Beatles, superstars from the past, are well on their way to becoming vintage.

Their four personalities were markedly different to begin with. For many years, they were managed by a master diplomat, a man with a plan, a visionary who realized a vision. In some ways, Epstein was a campaign manager without equal, but even he couldn't control the extraordinary circumstances which influenced four equally extraordinary lives, and only exacerbated the initial personality differences. Before Epstein died, it seems he knew that the empire had reached its fullest extent. From then on, it could only shrink.

After Epstein died, the Beatles became embroiled with money problems, and their subsequent guardians only embroiled them even further. The topic had never seemed to concern them during Epstein's regime. As Derek Taylor said: "Epstein was very clever at putting over the Beatles and making it seem that they weren't interested in money." The world just assumed that they were rich beyond belief. Suddenly they discovered that they had to concern themselves with this mundane problem. Then the world saw them not as saviors, but as four rather bloated myths.

They made desperate attempts to cling to their mansions and Rolls-Royces, after they discovered that many of their so-called friends had milked them. Then the business establishment at large began to take an interest in their dwindling fortune. Their cries for help were heeded by equally hardheaded businessmen, who saw an opportunity to get inside the gold mine and hack away. It is ironic that even now the Beatles fail to see that these new guardians had motives no different from the people they were brought in to fight. Their fortune was trimmed and their image was shattered; only their music remained. Strangely enough, it was Sir Lew Grade who said: "Those songs in Northern will live on forever."

New York,
September 8, 1971

ABOUT THE AUTHORS

PETER MCCABE was born in Liverpool, England, in 1945 and was graduated from Cambridge University. He subsequently worked as a staff correspondent for Reuters news service in Europe and the United States and as an editor of *Rolling Stone Magazine*. He now resides in New York City.

ROBERT D. SCHONFELD attended Kenyon College where he received a B.A. in political science. He has worked as a freelance photographer and a floor clerk on the New York Stock Exchange. He will receive his M.B.A. from New York University Graduate School of Business Administration this year.